Fu*k Them Turtles

The Illusion of Impact and How to Embrace Real Change

Frank Lazaro

Fu*k Them Turtles
The Illusion of Impact and How to Embrace Real Change

Copyright © 2024 by Frank Lazaro.

All rights reserved, including the right of reproduction in whole or in part in any form, except for brief quotations in printed reviews, without prior permission of the publisher.

Frank Lazaro LLC
www.franklazaro.com

Interior layout: Frank Lazaro

ISBN-13: 979-8-9887789-7-4
ePub ISBN: 979-8-9887789-8-1
PDF ISBN: 979-8-9887789-9-8

Some of the anecdotal illustrations in this book are true to life and are included with the permission of the people involved. All other
illustrations are composites of real situations, and any resemblance to people, living or dead, is coincidental.

First Printing, 2024

DEDICATION

To all the turtles: sea, teenage, ninja, or otherwise.

CONTENTS

1. Fu*k Them Turtles — 8
2. Why Do You Care? — 13
3. No Such Thing as Control — 26
4. What's the Story of You — 52
5. What Are You Going to Do Differently? — 74
6. Just Take a Step Forward — 94
7. Manifest Your Outcomes — 109
8. Ignore the Noise — 127
9. Become Your Own Champion — 150
10. Be Intentional — 172

1

FU*K THEM TURTLES

I guess the big question or the elephant in the room is, where does the book title come from? Fu*k Them Turtles. You are probably curious about what it means and how it relates to anything about improving yourself, your career, or whatever.

These are all good and valid questions. The phrase's origin comes from a conversation I was having with my twin boys, Evan and Hayden, when they were younger—maybe preteens. In a lot of ways, they are miniature versions of myself. I'm unsure if this is good or bad, yet here we are.

Anyway, we were having dinner out, and the restaurant

had paper straws. Just reading that sentence, you probably had a visceral reaction. You either supported it, or you downright hated it. There is no in-between – love or hate. However, I do not know of anyone that loves paper straws.

Anyway, our conversation went off the rails, as so many of our conversations do. Still, I commented that plastic straws were fundamentally better than paper ones and did not matter, so fu*k them turtles. It was a joke, and I was just being a dad trying to be funny.

But it had a deeper meaning the more I thought about it. Why didn't it matter? Because we (like everyone in the world) do it, or it does not work. And one random restaurant in Atlanta will not change a thing.

But let's examine this seemingly flippant remark more closely and consider how it relates to the broader themes of this book.

The phrase "Fu*k Them Turtles" has evolved for me into a metaphor for a more significant, more profound lesson about change, impact, and the human condition. It encapsulates the frustration and futility we often feel when faced with societal pressures, the paradoxes of modern life, or even the paradoxes at work. Here is the real takeaway: it is about recognizing the futility of token gestures when they are not backed by systemic change, collective effort, or intentionality.

It is the illusion of impact. In the case of paper straws, it represents the small, often performative actions that are meant to show we are contributing to a cause. While the intention behind using paper straws is noble—aiming to reduce plastic waste and save marine life—the reality is that unless this action is part of a more significant, more cohesive effort, its impact is negligible. Understanding that real, meaningful change requires more than surface-level actions. It is about the necessity for profound, systemic changes rather than superficial fixes.

However, relating this to personal and professional growth, this concept extends directly to personal and professional development. How often do we find ourselves engaging in activities that feel productive but do not lead to significant progress?

We attend workshops, read self-help books, and follow the latest trends, believing these will transform our lives. However, without a more profound commitment and a strategic approach, these actions are as effective as swapping a plastic straw for a paper one. They may feel good in the moment but do not drive real change.

But what about collective responsibility? Another layer to "Fu*k Them Turtles" is the notion of collective responsibility. True progress and improvement—whether in environmental conservation, personal growth, or professional success—require collective action and responsibility. It is not enough for one person or a small group to make a change if the rest are not on board. This is true in a corporate setting as well. One team's efforts can be undermined if the organization is not aligned with the same goals and values.

This means breaking free from perfectionism, so the title also challenges the notion of perfectionism and the pressure to do everything flawlessly. In our pursuit of excellence, we often become paralyzed by the fear of making the wrong choice or not making enough of a difference. "Fu*k Them Turtles" is a call to action to move beyond this paralysis, focus on impactful changes, and not be bogged down by pursuing perfect but inconsequential actions.

What are the practical takeaways? What does this mean for you, the reader? It means focusing on what truly matters and what will create real, lasting change in your life and career. It means not getting sidetracked by the small, symbolic gestures that make you feel good but do not move the needle. It is about making decisions with significant impacts, prioritizing actions that lead to substantial growth, and pushing beyond the easy wins to tackle the more challenging but rewarding tasks.

"Fu*k Them Turtles" is about stripping away the distractions and focusing on what will make a difference. It is about recognizing the bigger picture and understanding that meaningful change comes from concerted, collective efforts and concentrating on substantial, impactful actions.

As you read this book, keep this mindset in mind. Challenge yourself to surpass the easy, superficial fixes and strive for more profound, significant changes. That is where real growth happens and how you can make a true impact.

2

WHY DO YOU CARE?

One of the questions I ask when coaching someone or if someone comes to me with a problem unrelated to them, their work, or their department is: Why do you care? The question sounds cold and maybe even mean, but it has actual power.

This question aims to get the person to think about why it matters and whether their energy should be directed towards something they can control or something that matters.

We often focus on what others are doing or how they do it. But at the end of the day, if it is not your project, it is not your problem. No one cares that you would do it differently or that they are doing it wrong. Granted, there are exceptions if you are also on that project or it directly impacts you, but far too often, we worry ourselves about things we should not care about.

It comes down to the power of focus. The central theme here is focus. Focusing on what truly matters to you is an invaluable skill in a world filled with distractions and endless opportunities to weigh in on other people's issues. By asking, "Why do you care?" you force yourself to evaluate whether the problem is worth your attention and energy. This helps you prioritize your tasks and align your efforts with your personal and professional goals.

So why is Focus so important? Focus is concentrating on a single point of interest, task, or goal with undivided attention. Today, where distractions are constant and ubiquitous, maintaining focus is a powerful skill distinguishing between success and mediocrity. Here's why focus is crucial.

Focus increases productivity. It is that simple. If you can focus, you can do more.

When you focus on a task, you can complete it more efficiently and effectively. Although multitasking is often praised, it leads to divided attention and lower-quality work. You enhance your productivity and output quality by dedicating your attention to one task at a time.

Focusing enhances decision-making—simply put, focus helps you make better decisions. When you are clear about your priorities, you can evaluate options and make choices that align with your goals. This clarity reduces the noise and confusion that often accompany decision-making processes.

It also helps you build momentum, but how? Consistent focus on your goals creates momentum. Each completed task or achieved milestone builds on the previous one, driving you forward and making it easier to sustain your progress over time. This momentum is essential for long-term success.

One unexpected outcome of focus is it reduces stress. Distractions and multitasking can lead to feelings of overwhelm and stress. Focusing on one task at a time allows you to manage your workload more effectively and reduce the stress of juggling multiple responsibilities.

Deep focus allows you to immerse yourself fully in your work, leading to higher-quality outcomes. Whether writing a report, developing a new strategy, or learning a new skill, focused attention enables you to perform at your best.

We cannot forget the role of focus in prioritization and

ask ourselves, "Why do you care?" You harness the power of focus to evaluate and prioritize your tasks. This question forces you to scrutinize whether an issue deserves your time and energy. Here's how focus aids in prioritization:

Focus helps you align your activities with your personal and professional goals. Concentrating on tasks that directly contribute to your objectives ensures that your efforts always move you closer to your desired outcomes.

Focusing helps with filtering out noise. In a world of distractions, focus is a filter separating important tasks from trivial ones. It enables you to identify which activities add value and are merely distractions, allowing you to invest your energy where it matters most.

Practical focus improves time management skills. Concentrating on high-priority tasks makes better use of time, avoids procrastination, and ensures that critical deadlines are met.

Do you want to increase your engagement? Focus. When you focus on tasks that matter, your engagement and commitment levels rise. This increased engagement leads to higher motivation, better performance, and greater satisfaction in your work.

What are the strategies to improve focus? Set Clear Goals. Clearly defined goals provide a roadmap for your focus. Staying on track and avoiding distractions is easier when you know what you want to achieve.

It would be best to create a focused environment, designating a workspace without distractions. Use tools and techniques like time blocking, the Pomodoro Technique, or noise-canceling headphones to create an environment conducive to focus.

Another thing to do is practice mindfulness. This includes meditation and deep breathing, which can improve your concentration. These practices train your mind to stay present and reduce the impact of distractions.

Also, do not forget to limit multitasking - Focus on one task at a time. Complete it before moving on to the next. This approach reduces cognitive load and enhances the quality of your work.

It is also essential to take regular breaks. Short breaks between tasks can help maintain elevated levels of focus and prevent burnout. Use breaks to recharge and return to your work with renewed energy.

In the end, focus is a powerful theme because it underpins productivity, decision-making, and overall success. Ask yourself, "Why do you care?" You harness the power of focus to evaluate and prioritize your tasks, ensuring your efforts align with your goals. In a world filled with distractions, maintaining focus on what truly matters is an invaluable skill that can significantly enhance your personal and professional life.

Developing and nurturing this skill requires intentional practice and dedication, but the rewards are well worth the effort. By focusing on what matters most, you can achieve your goals more efficiently, produce higher quality work, and experience greater satisfaction in your accomplishments.

With that, you need emotional and mental clarity. Caring about every problem you encounter or hear about can lead to emotional and mental exhaustion. By constantly involving yourself in matters that do not directly affect you, you spread your emotional resources too thin, making it harder to deal with the issues that matter. Asking, "Why do you care?" serves as a filter, allowing you to preserve your mental and emotional bandwidth for the challenges that genuinely need your attention.

So why is emotional and mental clarity important? In

today's interconnected world, we are constantly bombarded with information, opinions, and problems from all directions. It is easy to become overwhelmed and emotionally drained by caring about every issue that comes our way. Emotional and mental clarity are crucial for maintaining well-being, productivity, and focus. But are they essential? The answer is yes.

It prevents emotional exhaustion. Caring deeply about multiple issues simultaneously can lead to emotional exhaustion, which occurs when you feel overwhelmed and drained by the demands placed on your emotional resources. Maintaining clarity about what truly matters to you can prevent burnout and preserve your emotional health.

Further, it enhances decision-making - Emotional and mental clarity allow you to make better decisions. When your mind is cluttered with too many concerns, it is challenging to think clearly and make rational choices. Clarity helps you weigh your options, consider the consequences, and choose the best action.

A clear mind is more focused and productive - Improves Focus and Productivity. When you filter out unnecessary concerns, you can concentrate on the tasks and challenges directly impacting your goals. This focus leads to higher efficiency and better outcomes.

It also supports emotional resilience; your emotional clarity helps you build resilience. By managing your emotional resources wisely, you are better equipped to handle stress and bounce back from setbacks. Resilience is crucial for maintaining long-term well-being and achieving your goals.

Mental clarity is vital for overall mental health, promoting mental well-being. A cluttered mind can contribute to anxiety, stress, and even depression. You can maintain a healthier, more balanced mental state by filtering out distractions and focusing on what truly matters.

What are the strategies for achieving emotional and mental clarity? First, practice mindfulness.

Mindfulness practices, such as meditation, yoga, and deep breathing exercises, can help you achieve emotional and mental clarity. These practices train your mind to stay present and reduce the impact of stress and distractions.

Next, set boundaries and establish clear boundaries around your time and emotional energy. Learn to say no to tasks and issues that do not align with your priorities.

This helps protect your emotional resources and ensures you are not overwhelmed by external demands.

It is important to prioritize self-care. Engage in activities that rejuvenate your mind and body, such as exercise, hobbies, and spending time with loved ones. Self-care practices help you recharge and maintain emotional balance.

Next, be selective about the information you consume. Avoid overexposure to news and social media, which can contribute to mental clutter and anxiety. Focus on sources that provide value and support your goals.

While I struggle with this, reflecting and journaling can be helpful. Regular reflection and journaling can help you process your thoughts and emotions. Writing down your concerns, goals, and achievements provides clarity and perspective, allowing you to manage your emotional and mental resources more effectively.

It would not be me if I did not try to tie it back to some real-world examples.

Workplace Focus: Imagine you are a manager responsible for leading a team. You hear about issues in other departments, but these do not directly affect your team's performance. By asking yourself, "Why do you care?" You can filter out these distractions and focus on supporting your team and achieving your department's goals.

Personal Relationships: In personal relationships, you might feel compelled to mediate conflicts or solve problems for friends and family. While it is essential to be supportive, constantly involving yourself in others' issues can lead to emotional exhaustion. Maintaining clarity about your boundaries allows you to offer help without depleting your emotional resources.

Community Involvement: If you are active in community service, you might encounter numerous causes and issues that need attention. It is easy to become overwhelmed by trying to address all of them. You can contribute effectively without burning out by focusing on the causes that align with your values and where you can make the most impact.

Emotional and mental clarity are essential for navigating the complexities of modern life. By asking, "Why do you care?" You can filter out unnecessary concerns and focus on what truly matters. This clarity prevents emotional exhaustion, enhances decision-making, improves productivity, supports resilience, and promotes mental well-being.

Achieving emotional and mental clarity requires intentional effort and practice. You can maintain a clear mind and a balanced emotional state by incorporating mindfulness, setting boundaries, prioritizing self-care, limiting information overload, and reflecting regularly. This clarity empowers you to invest your energy in the challenges that matter most, leading to a more fulfilling and successful personal and professional life.

A common theme throughout this book is the Illusion of Control. Our concern for external issues often stems from a desire to control our environment. However, controlling things beyond our reach only leads to frustration and a sense of helplessness. By focusing on what you can control—your actions, your projects, your responsibilities—you empower yourself to make meaningful changes and improvements. This shift in focus from external to internal control is crucial for personal and professional growth.

It would be best if you focused on productive engagement. When you ask yourself, "Why do you care?" You also pave the way for more fruitful engagement with your work and team. Instead of getting bogged down by every issue that crosses your path, you can channel your efforts towards projects and problems where you can make a tangible impact. This improves your productivity and enhances your sense of accomplishment and job satisfaction.

This then leads to setting boundaries. Another important aspect of this question is setting boundaries. Getting pulled into many issues that do not necessarily require your involvement is easy in professional settings. Setting clear boundaries about what you will and will not engage in protects your time and energy, allowing you to focus on your key responsibilities and goals. This also helps manage stress and avoid burnout.

What is the practical application of this so far? To illustrate this point, let us consider a few scenarios:

Office Gossip: Imagine you overhear colleagues discussing a departmental change that does not affect your team. Instead of getting involved and spending your mental energy on gossip, ask yourself, "Why do I care?" If the change does not impact your work, staying focused on your tasks is better.

Project Mismanagement: You notice another team is struggling with project management. Unless you are part of that team or your work is directly affected, intervening is not your place. Instead, focus on your projects and how you can improve your management skills.

Social Media Debates: Getting drawn into debates or controversies on social media can be a huge time-sink. Before engaging, ask yourself, "Why do I care?" Often, these debates do not lead to productive outcomes and can drain your energy and focus.

Asking "Why do you care?" is not about being indifferent or apathetic but about being strategic with your time and energy. It is about understanding where to make the most impact and focusing your efforts. By honing this skill, you can enhance your productivity, maintain emotional and mental clarity, and set healthy boundaries that protect you from unnecessary stress and distractions.

Ultimately, caring about the right things—not everything—is a key to personal and professional success. It is about directing your passion and energy towards what truly matters and letting go of what does not. So next time you find yourself getting worked up over something, pause and ask yourself why you care.

3

THERE IS NO SUCH THING AS CONTROL

In the previous chapter, we discussed the illusion of control and how our concern for external issues often stems from a desire to manage our environment. In a professional context, this desire can manifest in several ways, usually leading to frustration and a sense of helplessness when things do not go as planned. The reality is that control, as we often perceive it, is an illusion.

There is this myth of control. We are expected to encounter situations beyond our control in a work environment. These could be anything from organizational changes and market fluctuations to the actions of colleagues and clients. The belief that we can control these external factors can lead to undue stress and wasted effort. Recognizing that there is no such thing as complete control is the first step toward a more productive and satisfying professional life.

It would be best if you focused on what you can control. The key to thriving in a professional setting is to focus on what you can control: your actions, your projects, and your responsibilities. You can make meaningful changes and improvements by channeling your energy towards these areas. This shift from external to internal control is essential for personal and professional growth.

You can control your behavior, reactions to situations, and handling of challenges. By maintaining professionalism, staying calm under pressure, and being proactive, you set a positive example for others and contribute to a healthier work environment.

Expanding on this, let us dive deeper into how your actions can create a ripple effect in your professional and personal life.

It is essential to control your behavior and maintain professionalism, the cornerstone of a productive and respectful workplace. It involves adhering to workplace norms, demonstrating respect for colleagues, and fulfilling your duties with integrity. You build trust and credibility with your peers and superiors by consistently exhibiting professionalism.

Example: Always arriving on time for meetings, dressing appropriately, and following through on your commitments highlights your reliability and respect for others' time.

It is vital to stay calm under pressure. High-pressure situations are inevitable, but how you respond to them can significantly impact the outcome. Staying calm under pressure involves controlling your emotions, thinking clearly, and making rational decisions even when stressed.

Techniques: To help you stay composed, practice deep breathing, mindfulness, and time management skills. Regularly reflecting on past stressful situations and analyzing how you handled them can also provide valuable insights for future scenarios.

Example: During a critical project deadline, instead of panicking, break down the tasks into manageable parts, delegate effectively, and maintain open communication with your team to ensure smooth progress.

I cannot stress enough the importance of being proactive. Proactivity means anticipating potential challenges and acting before they become problems. It involves taking initiative, being forward-thinking, and consistently seeking ways to improve processes and outcomes.

Approach: Develop a habit of regularly reviewing your work and identifying areas for improvement. Stay informed about industry trends and changes impacting your role or organization.

Example: If you notice a project falling behind schedule, proactively suggest solutions such as reallocating resources, adjusting timelines, or seeking additional support to get back on track.

Next, handling challenges requires adaptive problem-solving skills. Challenges and obstacles are part of any professional journey. Your ability to adapt and solve problems efficiently determines your effectiveness and resilience.

Strategy: Approach problems with a solution-oriented mindset. Break down the issue, consider multiple perspectives, and brainstorm potential solutions. Engaging in creative thinking and collaborating with others can lead to innovative solutions.

Example: When faced with a technical glitch in a

crucial software tool, instead of getting frustrated, assess the situation, consult with IT support, and explore alternative tools or workarounds to keep the project moving forward.

Emotional intelligence (EI or EQ) is the ability to understand and manage your emotions and those of others. High EI helps you navigate social complexities, lead effectively, and build stronger relationships.

Components: Develop self-awareness, self-regulation, empathy, and social skills. Practice active listening, show empathy towards colleagues, and manage conflicts tactfully and diplomatically.

Example: If a team member struggles with their workload, approach the situation empathetically instead of reprimanding them. Offer support, provide constructive feedback, and help them find ways to manage their tasks more effectively.

Another way is to set a positive example and, more importantly, lead by example. Your behavior sets a standard for others to follow. By demonstrating professionalism, calmness, and proactivity, you inspire your colleagues to adopt similar attitudes and behaviors.

Leadership: Whether you hold a formal leadership

position or not, your actions can influence the team's dynamics and morale. Leading by example creates a culture of accountability, respect, and excellence.

Example: As a project leader, maintaining a positive attitude, even during setbacks, encourages your team to stay motivated and resilient. Acknowledging their efforts and celebrating successes fosters a supportive and collaborative environment.

We all know how a toxic work environment can ruin a culture, so building a positive work environment can help... Your actions contribute to the overall work environment. Positive behavior promotes a culture of respect, trust, and collaboration, leading to higher job satisfaction and productivity.

Culture: Encourage open communication, recognize and reward good work, and foster community within the team. A positive work environment reduces stress and enhances employee well-being.

Example: Implementing regular team-building activities, providing constructive feedback, and creating opportunities for professional growth help build a cohesive and engaged team.

While you may not control external circumstances, you

ultimately control your actions and reactions. Maintaining professionalism, staying calm under pressure, and being proactive enhance your effectiveness and positively influence those around you. Your ability to handle challenges gracefully and lead by example contributes significantly to creating a healthier, more productive work environment. Embrace the power of your actions and watch as they pave the way for a more prosperous and fulfilling professional journey.

If you apply this to your projects, while you might not control every aspect of a project, you can control your contribution. Focus on delivering high-quality work, meeting deadlines, and being a reliable team member. This will enhance your professional reputation and help you feel more empowered and in control of your work.

Understanding and managing your responsibilities is within your control. Prioritize your tasks, set realistic goals, and continuously seek ways to improve your efficiency and productivity. Doing so can achieve better outcomes and reduce the stress of feeling overwhelmed.

So, how do you deal with the uncontrollable? While focusing on what you can control is crucial, developing strategies for dealing with the uncontrollable aspects of your work life is equally important. Here are a few approaches:

Acceptance is a critical step in many things in life. Accept that there will always be elements outside your control. By acknowledging this fact, you can reduce the frustration and anxiety of managing the unmanageable.

Let's explore the concept of acceptance and its significance in personal and professional life.

First, we must understand acceptance. Acceptance is the recognition and acknowledgment of reality without resistance or denial. It involves understanding that certain factors are beyond your control and attempting to control them is futile. Embracing acceptance can lead to a more balanced and less stressful life.

Acceptance is crucial simply because it reduces stress and anxiety. Constantly trying to control the uncontrollable can lead to significant stress and anxiety. By accepting that some elements are beyond your influence, you free yourself from the mental and emotional burden of trying to manage everything. This acceptance allows you to focus on what you can control, thereby reducing overall stress levels.

When we think of emotional intelligence, a vital part is

enhancing your emotional resilience. Acceptance builds emotional resilience by helping you adapt to changes and challenges more effectively. Accepting setbacks and difficulties as a natural part of life makes you better equipped to handle them without becoming overwhelmed or discouraged.

Further, acceptance brings mental clarity by eliminating unnecessary worries and distractions. When you stop fixating on what you cannot change, your mind becomes more precise and focused on finding solutions for the aspects you can influence.

Another important outcome is that it fosters personal growth. Embracing acceptance encourages personal growth and self-awareness. It allows you to acknowledge and work within your limitations, leading to a more realistic and grounded approach to life. This mindset fosters continuous learning and development.

Again, I would like to learn through practical steps to help cultivate acceptance.

Where to start? Start by acknowledging your limits. Recognize and acknowledge the limits of your control. Understand that certain situations, such as the actions of others, external events, and natural occurrences, are beyond your influence. Accepting these limits helps you focus your energy on areas where you can make a difference.

Next is mindfulness, which involves being present in the moment and observing your thoughts and feelings without judgment. Practicing mindfulness helps you become more aware of your reactions to situations and cultivates a mindset of acceptance. Meditation, deep breathing, and mindful observation can be beneficial.

Once you are more aware or mindful, reframe Your Perspective. Reframe how you view challenges and setbacks. Instead of seeing them as obstacles, view them as opportunities for growth and learning. This shift in perspective helps you accept difficulties as part of the journey and reduces resistance to change.

After you are in the right state of mind, and I cannot say this enough, you must let go of perfectionism, which often leads to an excessive desire for control. Accept that perfection is unattainable, and that mistakes and imperfections are part of the human experience. Embracing imperfection allows you to approach life with greater flexibility and ease.

Focus on What You Can Control and direct your

energy and attention towards aspects you can control, such as your actions, attitudes, and responses. By concentrating on these areas, you can make meaningful progress and feel empowered and accomplished.

How does this play out in the real world? Here are some examples of acceptance.

Workplace Changes: Imagine your company undergoes a major restructuring, resulting in changes to your team and responsibilities. Instead of resisting the changes, accept them as part of the business's evolving nature. Focus on adapting to your new role and contributing effectively within the new structure.

Personal Relationships: In personal relationships, you may encounter behaviors or decisions from loved ones that you cannot control. Acceptance involves recognizing that you cannot change others but can choose how you respond to them. By accepting their autonomy, you can foster healthier and more respectful relationships.

Health Challenges: Facing health challenges, whether you or those of a loved one, can be tough. Acceptance means acknowledging the reality of the situation and focusing on what can be done to manage it. This might involve seeking medical advice, making lifestyle adjustments, and finding emotional support.

Pivoting to the benefits of acceptance in professional life, what could be the potential impacts?

Improved Team Dynamics: Acceptance promotes a healthier work environment by reducing conflicts and fostering collaboration. When team members accept each other's strengths and weaknesses, they can work together more effectively and build a supportive culture.

Enhanced Leadership: Leaders who practice acceptance demonstrate emotional intelligence and resilience. They acknowledge their teams' uncertainties and challenges and guide them. This approach builds trust and inspires confidence among team members.

Acceptance encourages a culture of experimentation and innovation. When employees feel safe taking risks and making mistakes without fear of harsh judgment, they are more likely to explore creative solutions and contribute innovative ideas.

Acceptance is a powerful tool for managing life's complexities and uncertainties. You can reduce frustration, stress, and anxiety by recognizing and acknowledging the elements outside your control. Cultivating acceptance enhances emotional resilience, promotes mental clarity, and fosters personal and professional growth.

Incorporating acceptance into your daily life involves acknowledging your limits, practicing mindfulness, reframing your perspective, letting go of perfectionism, and focusing on what you can control. This mindset improves well-being and creates a more positive and productive work environment.

Embrace acceptance as a guiding principle, and watch as it transforms your approach to challenges, enhances your relationships, and leads to a more balanced and fulfilling life.

Another key to success is adaptability and developing the ability to adapt to changing circumstances. This means being flexible, open to new ideas, and willing to adjust your plans when necessary. Adaptability is a valuable skill that can help you navigate uncertainty and stay resilient in facing challenges.

Expanding on this, let us explore the deeper facets of adaptability and why it is crucial for personal and professional success.

Let us start by understanding what adaptability is and is not. Adaptability is the capacity to adjust one's thoughts, behaviors, and actions in response to new or unexpected situations. It involves a combination of flexibility, resilience, and a proactive mindset. Adaptability allows one to thrive in dynamic environments and overcome obstacles gracefully and efficiently.

Why is adaptability crucial to your professional and personal growth? First, we all need to learn to navigate uncertainty. Everything today moves so fast, and change is constant. Industries evolve, technologies advance, and unforeseen challenges arise. Adaptability equips you with the skills to navigate these uncertainties effectively, ensuring you remain productive and focused regardless of external shifts.

I would focus on enhancing problem-solving skills; adaptable individuals are better problem-solvers. They can think on their feet, consider various perspectives, and develop creative solutions. This flexibility in thinking allows them to tackle complex problems more effectively than those who are rigid in their approach.

This is a common theme in this book, but resilience is a cornerstone. Adaptability enhances resilience by fostering a positive attitude toward change. Resilient individuals view challenges as opportunities for growth rather than threats. This mindset enables them to recover quickly from setbacks and maintain their momentum.

We all think we are innovative, and adaptability fosters innovation. Being open to new ideas and willing to adjust plans encourages innovation. Adaptable individuals are unafraid to experiment, take risks, and explore uncharted territories. This openness leads to breakthroughs and advancements that can drive personal and professional growth.

We all must embrace change and view change as an opportunity rather than a threat. Train yourself to see the potential benefits of change, such as new experiences, skills, and perspectives.

This requires us to cultivate a growth mindset and, by adopting a growth mindset, focus on learning and development. It would be best if you believed that you could improve your abilities through effort and practice. This mindset helps you stay open to new challenges and persist in facing difficulties.

Knowledge is power, isn't that what they say? It would be best if you stayed informed. Keep up with industry trends, technological advancements, and global events. Staying informed helps you anticipate changes and prepare for them. This proactive approach reduces sudden changes' shock and allows smoother transitions.

Being informed is one thing, but learning continuously is a game-changer. Commit to lifelong learning. Take courses, attend workshops, and seek new experiences that expand your knowledge and skills. Continuous learning keeps you adaptable and ready to tackle new challenges.

If something is too rigid, it will break. If you accept that you will not always get what you want and can be flexible, you will be better off, so practice flexibility.

Flexibility involves being willing to alter your plans and strategies when necessary. Practice flexibility by regularly evaluating and adjusting your goals based on new information and changing circumstances.

Everyone wants feedback until they get it, which is hard for many people. However, it is important to seek input.

Regularly seek feedback from peers, mentors, and supervisors. Constructive feedback provides insights into areas where you can improve and adapt. Use this feedback to refine your approach and enhance your adaptability.

What are some real-world Examples of adaptability? Let us start with workplace dynamics. Imagine your company implementing a new software system. Instead of resisting the change, embrace it by learning how to use the new system efficiently. Attend training sessions, ask questions, and experiment with the latest tools. Your adaptability makes the transition smoother and sets a positive example for your colleagues.

Another is career transitions; we all will change jobs at some point – some on purpose, and others will be forced upon us.

If you are transitioning to a new industry, adaptability is critical. Research the industry, identify transferable skills, and be open to learning new ones. Network with professionals in the field to gain insights and adjust your career plans based on the information you gather.

Unbelievably, we are all project managers, formal or informal. You may face unexpected challenges as a project manager, such as resource shortages or changing client requirements. Adaptability involves reassessing the project plan, reallocating resources, and communicating changes effectively to your team. This proactive approach ensures project success despite obstacles.

Let us now consider the benefits of adaptability in professional life. Immediately, the one that stands out is increased employability.

Employers value adaptable employees who can handle change and thrive in dynamic environments. Demonstrating adaptability can make you more attractive to potential employers and increase your career opportunities.

Adaptable individuals contribute positively to team dynamics. They are open to different viewpoints, willing to compromise, and can navigate conflicts effectively. This fosters a collaborative and productive work environment.

Adaptability is critical to your leadership development if you want to develop as a leader.

Adaptability is a crucial trait of influential leaders. Leaders who can adapt to changing circumstances inspire confidence in their teams and guide them through uncertainty. This ability to lead through change enhances your leadership potential and career advancement prospects.

Adaptability is essential in a world where change is the only constant. By developing the ability to adapt to changing circumstances, you equip yourself with the tools needed to navigate uncertainty and stay resilient in the face of challenges. To enhance your adaptability, embrace change, cultivate a growth mindset, stay informed, learn continuously, practice flexibility, and seek feedback.

Remember, the most successful individuals can adapt quickly and efficiently to new situations. By being adaptable, you improve your effectiveness and contribute positively to your team and organization. Embrace adaptability as a core principle and watch as it transforms your approach to challenges, paving the way for a more prosperous and fulfilling professional journey.

While you may not control everything, you can often influence outcomes through effective communication and collaboration. Build strong relationships with colleagues and stakeholders and use your influence to steer projects and decisions in a positive direction.

But let us explore why influence is significant and how to leverage it effectively to achieve desired outcomes.

What is the importance of influence? What does it do for us? First, there is enhanced collaboration.

Influence fosters collaboration and teamwork. Building strong relationships and effectively communicating your ideas can unite people to work towards common goals. This collaboration leads to more innovative solutions and better project outcomes.

When you effectively influence others, you can steer projects and decisions in a direction that aligns with your values and objectives. This capability is crucial for driving positive organizational change, improving processes, and achieving strategic goals.

Influence is built on trust and credibility. You earn your colleagues' and stakeholders' respect and trust by consistently demonstrating your expertise, reliability, and integrity. This trust makes persuading others and gaining their support for your initiatives easier.

Influence allows you to extend your impact beyond your immediate responsibilities. By guiding and inspiring others, you contribute to the overall success of your team and organization. This broader impact enhances your professional reputation and opens new opportunities for growth and advancement.

This is great, so let's discuss strategies for effective influence. First, it helps build and develop strong relationships.

Building solid and genuine relationships with colleagues and stakeholders is the foundation of influence. Take the time to understand their perspectives, needs, and motivations. Show empathy and support for their goals and build mutual respect through consistent and positive interactions.

Example: Regularly engage with your team members and stakeholders through one-on-one meetings, informal check-ins, and team-building activities. These interactions help you build rapport and trust, making it easier to influence them when needed.

Clear and persuasive communication is critical to influencing others. Articulate your ideas and recommendations in a compelling and easy-to-understand way. Use data, stories, and examples to support your points and make your message more impactful.

Example: When proposing a new project, prepare a well-structured presentation highlighting the benefits, potential challenges, and solutions. Use visuals and real-world examples to make your case more convincing and relatable.

Establish yourself as a knowledgeable and reliable expert in your field. Share your insights, stay informed about industry trends, and continuously develop your skills. When others recognize your expertise, they are more likely to value your opinions and follow your recommendations.

Example: Publish articles, give presentations, or lead workshops on topics related to your expertise. You can build credibility and influence within your organization and industry by showcasing your knowledge.

Influence is not about dominating discussions or imposing your views. It is about working collaboratively to achieve the best outcomes. Encourage open dialogue, listen actively to others' ideas, and incorporate their input into your plans. This inclusive approach fosters a sense of ownership and commitment among team members.

Example: During team meetings, invite input from all participants and acknowledge their contributions. Use consensus-building techniques to develop strategies that reflect the group's collective wisdom.

Emotional intelligence (EI) involves understanding and managing your emotions and those of others. High EI helps you navigate social interactions more effectively, build stronger relationships, and influence others with empathy and sensitivity.

Example: Pay attention to the emotional cues of your colleagues and stakeholders. Respond with empathy and adjust your communication style to meet their emotional needs. For instance, if a team member feels stressed, offer support and reassurance rather than push for immediate decisions.

Influence often requires persistence and resilience. Not all your efforts will be successful immediately, and you may face resistance or setbacks. Stay committed to your goals, build relationships, and adapt your strategies.

Example: If your initial proposal is rejected, seek feedback to understand why. Use this information to refine your approach and present a revised plan that addresses the concerns raised.

As with most things in this book, we have to discuss real-world examples of influence, and there is no better place to start than with Project Management.

As a project manager, you may need to secure buy-in from various stakeholders to ensure project success. By building strong relationships, communicating effectively, and demonstrating the value of your project, you can influence stakeholders to support your initiatives and provide the necessary resources.

Example: When leading a cross-functional project, hold regular stakeholder meetings to update them on progress, address concerns, and gather input. Use these interactions to build trust and ensure alignment with project goals.

Another area it impacts is team leadership.

As a team leader, you can influence your team's performance and morale by setting a positive example, providing clear direction, and fostering a collaborative environment. Your influence helps create a culture of accountability, innovation, and continuous improvement.

Example: Encourage team members to share their ideas and take ownership of their tasks. Recognize and celebrate their achievements and provide constructive feedback to help them grow and succeed.

Finally, there is organizational change. Influence is crucial when advocating for organizational change, such as implementing a new process or technology. You can steer the organization toward successful adoption and integration of the change by effectively communicating the benefits, addressing concerns, and involving key stakeholders in decision-making.

Example: Develop a change management plan that includes stakeholder engagement, communication strategies, and training programs. Use this plan to guide the organization through the transition and ensure buy-in from all levels.

Again, touching on the practical applications to put these concepts into practice, think about these areas:

Organizational Changes: When your company undergoes a restructuring or a shift in strategy, focus on how you can adapt to the new environment. Instead of resisting change, look for opportunities to contribute and grow within the new framework.

Team Dynamics: If a team member's performance affects the project, concentrate on what you can do to support the team. This could involve helping, providing constructive feedback, or resolving the issue without derailing your progress.

Market Fluctuations: In industries susceptible to market changes, focusing on your response rather than the fluctuations themselves is essential. Stay informed, adjust your strategies proactively, and concentrate on areas where you can maintain stability and drive growth.

In the work environment, the concept of control is a myth. While it is natural to want to manage every aspect of your environment, many factors will always be beyond your reach. By focusing on what you can control—your actions, projects, and responsibilities—you empower yourself to make meaningful changes and improvements.

Simultaneously, developing strategies to cope with uncontrollable elements—such as acceptance, adaptability, and influence—can help you navigate the complexities of your work life more effectively. Embrace the idea that there is no such thing as complete control and shift your focus to where it truly matters. This approach will enhance your professional growth and lead to a more satisfying and less stressful career.

While you may not control every aspect of your environment, you can significantly influence outcomes through effective communication and collaboration. You can steer projects and decisions in a positive direction by building solid relationships, demonstrating expertise, and fostering a collaborative and empathetic approach.

Influence is a powerful tool that enhances collaboration, drives positive change, and expands your organizational impact. Embrace the above strategies to develop and leverage your influence, and watch as they transform your professional journey and contribute to your success.

4

WHAT'S THE STORY OF YOU

Professionally, one of the most powerful tools you possess is the ability to control your story. Your story is how people see you, how you present yourself, and how you navigate your career. This chapter is about understanding that you can shape your narrative and influence others to perceive you.

It comes down to the power of attitude. Every day, you have the choice to control your attitude. This is a fundamental aspect of your story. A positive, proactive attitude can set the tone for how you are perceived by colleagues, superiors, and even clients. It is about deciding each day to approach challenges with optimism and resilience, shaping your professional persona.

But how do you craft your narrative, and how do you sell yourself? How do you tell your story in a way that aligns with your goals and aspirations? Your narrative should be clear, consistent, and reflective of your values and capabilities. Here are some key elements to consider when crafting your story.

It is essential to start by identifying your core values. What principles drive you? Understanding your core values helps create an authentic and resonant story. Whether it is integrity, innovation, or teamwork, these values should be evident in how you present yourself.

Identifying your core values is a foundational step in crafting your narrative. Your core values are the guiding principles that shape your decisions, actions, and interactions. These values, whether integrity, innovation, teamwork, or others, are the compass that directs your professional and personal life. Understanding and articulating your core values helps create an authentic and resonant story. Here is why this is crucial:

Authenticity Builds Trust: When you operate from a place of authenticity, people are more likely to trust and respect you. Authenticity means that your actions and words are consistent with your values and beliefs. This congruence reassures others that you are genuine and reliable. Trust is the cornerstone of effective relationships with colleagues, clients, or superiors.

Enhances Connection. Authenticity allows you to connect on a deeper level with others. When you share your true self, including your values and what drives you, it resonates with people who share similar beliefs or appreciate your sincerity. This connection fosters more robust, meaningful relationships, essential for both personal satisfaction and professional success.

Guides Decision-Making. Clear core values provide a framework for making decisions. In moments of uncertainty or ethical dilemmas, your values serve as a reference point, helping you choose actions that align with your principles. This consistency in decision-making builds a reputation for integrity and dependability.

Drives Motivation and Engagement. When your work and actions are aligned with your core values, you are more likely to feel motivated and engaged. This alignment brings a sense of purpose and fulfillment, driving you to perform at your best. Staying committed and passionate about your work is easier when it reflects your beliefs.

Differentiates You from Others. Your core values can set you apart. They highlight what makes you unique and can be a defining factor in your brand. Employers, colleagues, and clients are not just looking for skills and experience but also for individuals whose values align with their organizational culture and goals.

Consistency and Reliability. Being true to your core values means you act consistently in various situations, which makes you more predictable and reliable. People appreciate knowing what to expect from you, strengthening your professional relationships, and enhancing your reputation.

Promotes Long-Term Success. Aligning your career with your core values contributes to long-term success and satisfaction. When your work environment and role are in harmony with your values, it reduces stress and increases your overall well-being, leading to sustained productivity and career growth.

Identifying and living by your core values is about self-awareness and creating a foundation for authenticity that permeates your professional narrative. This authenticity builds trust, enhances connections, guides decisions, drives motivation, differentiates you, ensures consistency, and promotes long-term success. By being authentic and transparent about your values, you craft a compelling and resonant story that reflects who you are and resonates deeply with others.

Focus on your unique strengths and how they have contributed to your past successes. Be specific about your skills and experiences that set you apart. This will not only build credibility but also make your story compelling.

Highlighting your strengths is essential in crafting a compelling personal narrative. Focusing on your unique strengths and how they have contributed to your past successes builds credibility and makes your story engaging and persuasive. Your strengths are the distinctive skills and attributes that set you apart. You demonstrate your value and potential impact by being specific about these strengths and providing concrete examples.

When you emphasize your strengths, you clearly show what you bring. This specificity helps others understand your capabilities and how you can contribute to their goals or projects. For instance, if you have a knack for strategic thinking, illustrate this by discussing a successful project where your strategic insights led to significant achievements. You are not just telling but showing your audience the tangible results of your strengths.

Focusing on your strengths allows you to present yourself confidently. Confidence is attractive and reassuring to potential employers, clients, or collaborators. It signals that you are aware of your abilities and comfortable leveraging them to achieve results. This self-assurance can inspire confidence in others, making them more likely to trust and support you.

Highlighting your strengths also enables you to craft a narrative that aligns with your career goals. You can position yourself as the ideal candidate by showcasing the skills and experiences most relevant to the roles or opportunities you seek. This targeted approach ensures your story resonates with your audience and meets their needs or expectations.

Additionally, reflecting on your strengths can help you identify patterns in your career that you may not have noticed before. Recognizing how your strengths have consistently contributed to your success can provide valuable insights into your professional identity and potential future paths. This self-awareness can guide you in making strategic career decisions that match your strengths and maximize your potential.

Highlighting your strengths is a powerful way to build a compelling personal narrative. It showcases your unique capabilities, demonstrates your value through specific examples, and aligns your story with your career goals. By confidently presenting your strengths, you build credibility and create an authentic narrative that resonates deeply with your audience. This approach ensures that your professional story is impactful and memorable, setting you apart in a competitive landscape.

Showcase Your Achievements: You need to use your accomplishments to illustrate your capabilities and understand how those capabilities are transferrable to other industries, departments, or companies. Highlight critical projects, awards, or milestones demonstrating your expertise and dedication. This adds concrete evidence to your narrative.

There is nothing wrong with reinventing yourself. Switching industries or roles can be daunting, but it also allows you to reinvent yourself. The key is to align your story with the new role you are pursuing.

Reinventing yourself by switching industries or roles can be daunting, but it also presents a valuable opportunity for growth and transformation. This process allows you to redefine your professional identity and align your narrative with your new path. The key to a successful reinvention lies in crafting a story that bridges your past experiences with your future aspirations.

One of the first steps in reinventing yourself is to identify the transferable skills that can apply across different industries or roles. These skills are the common threads that link your past to your desired future, showcasing your adaptability and versatility. For instance, if you excelled in project management in your previous role, highlight how those organizational and leadership skills can drive success in a new industry. Drawing these connections demonstrates that your core competencies remain valuable, even in a different context.

In addition to identifying transferable skills, it is crucial to communicate a clear and compelling rationale for your transition. This involves articulating why you are making the switch and how your background uniquely positions you to succeed in the new role. Whether driven by a passion for the new field, a desire for personal growth, or a strategic career move, your reasoning should be woven into your narrative. This helps others understand your motivations and see the logical progression of your career journey.

Another critical aspect of reinvention is continuous learning. Embrace the need to acquire new knowledge and skills relevant to your new industry or role. This proactive approach equips you with the necessary competencies and signals your commitment to growth and readiness to take on new challenges. Engaging in courses, certifications, and networking in the new field can provide valuable insights and connections to facilitate your transition.

Being open to change and maintaining a flexible mindset is essential when reinventing yourself. Change often brings uncertainty but also opportunities for innovation and creativity. By being adaptable and willing to step outside your comfort zone, you can navigate the challenges of a career switch with resilience and confidence.

It is also beneficial to seek out mentors or advisors who have successfully navigated similar transitions. Their guidance can provide valuable perspectives and practical advice, helping you avoid common pitfalls and accelerate your integration into the new industry or role. These mentors can also offer support and encouragement, reinforcing your confidence in succeeding.

Finally, communicating your reinvented story effectively is crucial. Update your resume, LinkedIn profile, and other professional platforms to reflect your new direction. Tailor your narrative to highlight the alignment between your achievements and future goals. This ensures that your story resonates with potential employers, clients, and colleagues, making it clear that you are capable and excited about the new opportunities ahead.

Reinventing yourself involves leveraging your transferable skills, articulating a clear rationale for your transition, embracing continuous learning, maintaining flexibility, seeking mentorship, and effectively communicating your new narrative. By aligning your story with your new role, you can successfully navigate the challenges of switching industries or roles, transforming potential obstacles into opportunities for growth and success. This approach enhances your professional journey and positions you as a dynamic and adaptable individual, ready to thrive in any environment. Here is how to do it effectively:

A key to reinventing yourself is translating your skills. Identify the transferable skills from your previous roles and articulate how they apply to the new industry. For example, if you have strong project management skills, explain how these can be utilized to manage complex projects in the new field.

Translating your skills is critical in successfully reinventing yourself when switching industries or roles. This process involves identifying the transferable skills from your previous experiences and effectively articulating how these skills are relevant and valuable in your new field. You can bridge the gap between your past and future, demonstrating your adaptability and readiness for new challenges.

Start by thoroughly assessing your previous roles and pinpointing the skills contributing to your success. Transferable skills are those abilities that are not specific to one industry but are universally applicable across various contexts. These often include competencies like project management, leadership, communication, problem-solving, and strategic planning. Identifying these skills helps you understand your core strengths in any role.

Once you clearly understand your transferable skills, the next step is to articulate their relevance to the new industry. This involves drawing clear connections between what you have done and your aim. For example, if you have strong project management skills from your previous role, highlight how these abilities can be applied to managing complex projects in your new field. Explain how your experience in coordinating teams, managing budgets, and meeting deadlines can directly contribute to the success of projects in your new industry.

Using specific examples and tangible results to illustrate your skills is essential. Instead of simply stating that you have project management experience, describe a significant project you managed successfully. Detail the challenges you faced, the actions you took, and the positive outcomes that resulted. This concrete evidence of your capabilities helps potential employers or clients see your value.

Additionally, tailor your language to resonate with your new industry. Every field has its terminology and preferred communication styles. By familiarizing yourself with these and incorporating them into your narrative, you demonstrate your understanding of the new industry's context and nuances. This shows you are capable and committed to seamlessly integrating into your new environment.

Networking and informational interviews can be valuable in this process. Speaking with professionals in your desired industry can provide insights into which of your skills are most relevant and how best to position them. These conversations can also reveal industry-specific challenges and opportunities, allowing you to tailor your narrative more effectively.

Consider any additional skills or knowledge you may need to enhance your transition. While your transferable skills provide a solid foundation, complementing them with industry-specific expertise can make you even more competitive. Enroll in relevant courses, attend workshops, or seek certifications that align with your new career goals. This proactive approach boosts your qualifications and demonstrates your commitment to continuous learning and professional development.

Translating your skills involves identifying your transferable abilities, articulating their relevance to the new industry, using specific examples to illustrate your expertise, tailoring your language to fit the new context, and complementing your skills with additional knowledge if necessary. By effectively communicating how your past experiences equip you for future success, you can make a compelling case for your ability to thrive in a new industry or role. This approach ensures that your narrative is convincing and impactful, positioning you as a versatile and valuable candidate ready to take on new challenges.

The key is connecting and leveraging your experiences. Draw parallels between your past experiences and the requirements of the new role. This shows you have the relevant background and can adapt to new challenges.

Leveraging your experiences is vital when transitioning to a new industry or role. By drawing parallels between your past experiences and the requirements of the new role, you demonstrate that you have a relevant background and the ability to adapt to new challenges. This approach helps potential employers or collaborators see your value and understand how your previous achievements translate into future success.

Start by conducting a thorough analysis of the new role's requirements. Understand the essential skills, competencies, and experiences needed to excel. Once you have a clear picture of the new role, reflect on your past experiences to identify situations where you have demonstrated these qualities. This alignment between your history and the new role's demands is crucial for making a persuasive case for your candidacy.

When drawing parallels, focus on specific examples highlighting your accomplishments and how they relate to the new position. For instance, if the new role requires strong leadership skills, discuss cases in which you successfully led teams, managed conflicts, or drove significant projects to completion. Emphasize the outcomes of your efforts, such as increased team productivity, successful project delivery, or enhanced team morale. These concrete examples provide evidence of your ability to meet the new role's expectations.

In addition to specific examples, consider the broader themes and patterns in your career. Identify recurring strengths and competencies that have consistently contributed to your success. These might include skills like strategic thinking, problem-solving, or adaptability. By showcasing these overarching themes, you create a narrative that underscores your capability to thrive in various environments and handle diverse challenges.

It is also essential to communicate your adaptability and learning agility. Highlight experiences where you successfully navigated change, learned new skills or adapted to different roles or industries. This demonstrates your ability to transition smoothly into the new role and quickly become effective. Employers value candidates who can hit the ground running and adapt to evolving circumstances.

When leveraging your experiences, be mindful of the language and terminology used in the new industry. Tailor your narrative by incorporating relevant jargon and concepts to resonate with the audience. This shows your understanding of the new field and helps bridge any perceived gaps between your past and future roles.

Networking and mentorship can also significantly influence this process. Engage with professionals with experience in the new industry to gain insights and advice on effectively positioning your background. Their guidance can help refine your narrative and ensure it aligns with industry expectations.

Additionally, consider any training or upskilling that might be beneficial. While your past experiences provide a solid foundation, enhancing your skill set with industry-specific knowledge can further bolster your candidacy. This proactive approach signals your commitment to growth and readiness to tackle new challenges.

Leveraging your experiences involves identifying and

articulating how your past achievements align with the requirements of the new role. Use specific examples to illustrate your relevant skills, highlight broader themes that underscore your strengths, and demonstrate your adaptability and learning agility. You create a compelling narrative that positions you as a capable and adaptable candidate by drawing parallels between your history and the new role's demands. This approach showcases your readiness for new challenges and reinforces your value in the eyes of potential employers or collaborators.

Be Clear and Consistent: Your story should convey why you are making the switch and how your past experiences make you a perfect fit for the new role. Consistency in your message across your resume, cover letter, and interviews is crucial.

You need to understand the role of attitude in Reinvention. Your attitude plays a significant role in how you reinvent yourself. Approach the transition with confidence and a willingness to learn. Emphasize your enthusiasm for the new industry and your commitment to bringing fresh perspectives. This positive attitude will be evident to potential employers and can influence their perception of you.

Practical Steps to Craft Your Story

Crafting your story might seem daunting, but it is straightforward and gratifying in many ways. Following practical steps, you can create a compelling and authentic narrative highlighting your unique strengths, experiences, and aspirations. The foundation of this process is self-assessment, a critical exercise in reflecting on your career journey, achievements, and the skills you have acquired.

Self-Assessment: Reflect on Your Career Journey

Begin with a thorough self-assessment. This involves taking time to reflect on your career path, the milestones you have achieved, and the skills you have developed. Consider the roles you have held, the projects you have completed, and the challenges you have overcome. Each of these elements contributes to your unique professional story.

Start by engaging in a thoughtful self-reflection. List your significant career experiences. What were the key projects or roles that left a lasting impact? Consider what you accomplished in these positions and the skills you utilized or developed. Reflect on the feedback you received and the outcomes of your efforts. This detailed examination helps you pinpoint the highlights of your career that you want to emphasize in your narrative.

Identify Your Achievements and Skills

Next, let's focus on your achievements. What are you most proud of? These achievements are not just milestones but the cornerstones of your professional story. They provide concrete evidence of your capabilities and successes. Be specific about the impact you made. For example, did you lead a team to complete a project under budget and ahead of schedule? Did you innovate a process that increased efficiency or customer satisfaction? Quantifiable results are particularly compelling as they demonstrate your value.

Alongside your achievements, identify the skills critical to your success. These skills can be technical, such as proficiency in a particular software, or soft skills, like leadership, communication, and problem-solving. Understanding these skills and how they have contributed to your achievements helps you articulate your strengths effectively.

Understand Your Core Values

Core values are the principles that drive you. They are the foundation of your authentic and resonant story. Whether it is integrity, innovation, teamwork, or another value, these should be evident in how you present yourself. Reflect on what matters most to you in your work and how these values have guided your decisions and actions. This authenticity builds trust and connection with your audience.

Create a Personal Brand Statement

Once you clearly understand your journey, achievements, skills, and values, distill this information into a personal brand statement. This statement should encapsulate who you are, what you do, and what makes you unique. It should be concise and memorable, serving as the cornerstone of your narrative. Your brand statement helps ensure consistency across all platforms where you share your story, from resumes and LinkedIn profiles to interviews and networking events.

Tailor Your Story for Different Audiences

While your core story remains the same, you may need to tailor it for different audiences. For instance, how you present your story in a job interview might differ slightly from how you describe it on your LinkedIn profile. Adjust the emphasis based on what is most relevant to the audience. This ensures that your story is always engaging and pertinent.

Practice Telling Your Story

Like any skill, effectively telling your story requires practice. Rehearse your narrative in various settings, such as networking events, interviews, or casual conversations. The more you practice, the more confident and natural you will become in sharing your story. This confidence can make a significant difference in how your story is received.

Seek Feedback

Finally, seek feedback from trusted mentors, colleagues, or professional coaches. They can provide valuable perspectives on how your story comes across and suggest improvements. Constructive feedback helps you refine your narrative, ensuring it is impactful and resonates with your audience.

Crafting your story involves a series of practical steps: conducting a thorough self-assessment, identifying your achievements and skills, understanding your core values, creating a personal brand statement, tailoring your story for different audiences, practicing your delivery, and seeking feedback. Following these steps, you can make a compelling and authentic narrative highlighting your unique professional journey and strengths. This well-crafted story enhances your brand and positions you for success in your career pursuits.

5

WHAT ARE YOU GOING TO DO DIFFERENTLY?

Change is inevitable if you want to achieve different results. The adage says it all: "You can't expect different results by doing the same thing," which is often attributed to Albert Einstein as the definition of insanity. This chapter touches on the importance of doing things differently to catalyze change in your personal and professional life.

It would be best to embrace change for growth—it is that simple. To grow and advance, you must be willing to step out of your comfort zone and embrace change. Whether starting your own consulting business, seeking a job promotion, or learning a new skill, success hinges on your ability to adapt and evolve. Here are key areas to consider.

Begin by assessing where you are currently and where you want to be. Clearly define your goals and identify the gaps between your current state and your desired future. This will help you pinpoint the areas where change is needed.

Self-assessment and goal setting are crucial steps in initiating meaningful change in your personal and professional life. To make progress, it is essential to begin by understanding your current position and envisioning where you want to be. By clearly defining your goals and identifying the gaps between your current state and your desired future, you can pinpoint the areas where change is necessary. This process lays the groundwork for strategic action and sustained growth.

Start with a thorough self-assessment. Reflect on your career journey, achievements, and the skills you have acquired. This is the foundation of your story, as discussed in Chapter 4. Consider your core values, which are crucial in guiding your decisions and actions. Understanding what drives you helps create an authentic and resonant narrative. Ask yourself: What are the principles that drive you? Whether it is integrity, innovation, or teamwork, these values should be evident in how you present yourself.

Next, identify your strengths and unique skills. Highlight the experiences that set you apart and have contributed to your past successes. Be specific about your skills and experiences, as this builds credibility and makes your story compelling. For instance, if you have strong project management skills, explain how these can be utilized to manage complex projects in a new field. Your ability to leverage your experiences and draw parallels between your past roles and the requirements of a new role demonstrates your capacity to adapt and succeed.

With a clear understanding of your current state, move on to goal setting. Define your goals using the SMART criteria: Specific, Measurable, Achievable, Relevant, and Time-bound. This clarity ensures that your goals are concrete and attainable. For example, instead of setting a vague goal like "I want to advance in my career," specify your aim: "I want to become a senior manager within the next two years by completing a leadership development program and leading a high-impact project."

Identifying the gaps between your current state and

your desired future is critical. This involves analyzing the skills, experiences, and knowledge you need to acquire to reach your goals. Reflect on the concept of reinventing yourself from Chapter 4. Switching industries or roles can be daunting, but it offers an opportunity to align your story with the new role you are pursuing. Understand the transferable skills from your previous roles and articulate how they apply to the latest industry. Draw parallels between your past experiences and the requirements of the new role to show that you have the relevant background and can adapt to new challenges.

Continuous learning and development are essential in bridging these gaps. Embrace growth opportunities through formal education, professional development courses, or practical experiences. Chapter 4 emphasized the importance of being open to change and maintaining a flexible mindset. This adaptability is crucial in navigating new challenges and acquiring the skills necessary for your desired future.

Leverage your experiences by seeking out stretch assignments and networking opportunities. These actions enhance your skill set and expand your professional network, opening doors to new possibilities and mentorship. Building relationships with professionals in your desired field can provide valuable insights and support as you work towards your goals.

Self-assessment and goal-setting are foundational steps in achieving meaningful change. By reflecting on your career journey, understanding your core values, highlighting your strengths, and setting clear, achievable goals, you can identify the areas where change is needed. Drawing on the principles and strategies discussed in earlier chapters, you can effectively bridge the gap between your current state and your desired future. This approach ensures your growth and success and aligns your actions with your long-term aspirations, paving the way for a fulfilling and impactful career.

One of the most effective ways to do things differently and drive meaningful change is by acquiring new knowledge and skills. In a rapidly evolving professional landscape, staying relevant and competitive requires a commitment to continuous learning. This dedication enhances your expertise and signals your commitment to personal and professional growth.

To start, enrolling in courses is a fundamental step. Look for courses relevant to your field or the new industry you are transitioning into. These courses can range from formal degree programs to short-term online classes. They provide structured learning environments to gain in-depth knowledge and practical skills. For instance, if you want to switch to a new industry, consider taking foundational courses covering that field's basics. This equips you with essential knowledge and shows potential employers you are serious about transitioning.

Attending workshops is another valuable approach to continuous learning. Workshops often offer hands-on experience and the opportunity to apply new real-life skills. They are typically shorter in duration than courses but can be equally impactful. Workshops also provide a platform for networking with professionals with similar interests or career goals. These connections can lead to further learning opportunities, collaborations, or mentorship.

Seeking relevant certifications is an excellent way to validate your skills and knowledge. Certifications are often recognized as industry standards, demonstrating your proficiency and commitment to staying current with industry trends and practices. For example, if you are in the IT sector, obtaining certifications like CompTIA,

CISSP, or AWS Certified Solutions Architect can significantly boost your credibility and career prospects. Similarly, project management certifications such as PMP (Project Management Professional) or Six Sigma can open doors to advanced roles and responsibilities.

Continuous learning goes beyond formal education and certifications. It also involves staying updated with your field's latest trends, technologies, and best practices. This can be achieved by regularly reading industry publications, participating in webinars, and engaging with professional communities on platforms like LinkedIn. Following thought leaders and industry experts can provide insights into emerging trends and innovative practices, keeping you ahead of the curve.

Learning should be seen as a lifelong journey. Adopting a growth mindset, as discussed in Chapter 4, is crucial. This mindset involves embracing challenges, learning from failures, and persisting in the face of setbacks. It encourages you to see every experience as an opportunity to learn and grow, fostering resilience and adaptability.

Continuous learning also demonstrates your commitment to growth. Employers and colleagues notice when you invest in your development. It signals that you are proactive, dedicated, and keen on contributing at a higher level. This commitment can set you apart in a competitive job market, making you a more attractive candidate for promotions, new roles, or challenging projects.

To integrate continuous learning into your routine, set specific learning goals. For instance, aim to complete a certain number of courses or certifications within a year, attend monthly workshops, or read several industry-related articles each week. Keeping track of your progress can provide a sense of accomplishment and motivate you to keep going.

Acquiring new knowledge and skills is essential for doing things differently and achieving your goals. By enrolling in courses, attending workshops, seeking relevant certifications, and continuously staying updated with industry trends, you enhance your expertise and demonstrate a strong commitment to growth. This proactive approach broadens your skill set and positions you as a dedicated and adaptable professional, ready to tackle new challenges and seize opportunities for advancement.

Working on stretch assignments can significantly impact your career trajectory by pushing you beyond your current capabilities. These assignments, often more complex and demanding than your usual tasks, provide a unique opportunity to develop new skills, gain valuable experience, and showcase your potential to senior management.

Stretch assignments force you out of your comfort zone, challenging you to tackle unfamiliar problems and navigate new responsibilities. This exposure to different aspects of your organization can broaden your understanding of the business and enhance your strategic thinking. By stepping into roles or projects that require skills beyond your current expertise, you demonstrate your willingness to learn and adapt, which is highly valued in any professional setting.

One key benefit of stretch assignments is skill development. These assignments often require you to acquire and apply new skills rapidly. Whether leading a cross-functional team, managing a high-stakes project, or developing a new business strategy, the hands-on experience you gain is invaluable. For example, a project management role can help you build leadership and organizational skills if you are typically involved in technical work. This diversifies your skill set and makes you more versatile and valuable to your organization.

Stretch assignments also provide an opportunity to gain visibility and recognition from senior management. Completing challenging projects demonstrates your capability and readiness for more significant responsibilities. It signals to leadership that you are proactive, capable of handling complexity, and willing to go the extra mile. This visibility is crucial for career advancement as it positions you as a potential candidate for promotions or leadership roles.

Stretch assignments allow you to build a track record of success in different areas of the business. This diverse experience can be a powerful addition to your resume, showcasing your ability to thrive in various contexts and handle diverse challenges. For instance, if you are an engineer who takes on a marketing project, you can demonstrate your ability to bridge technical and business domains, making you a more well-rounded professional.

To maximize the benefits of stretch assignments, approach them strategically. Set clear goals for what you want to achieve and the skills you wish to develop. Seek feedback regularly to understand your progress and areas for improvement. This feedback loop helps refine your approach and ensures you continuously learn and grow.

Collaboration is another critical aspect of succeeding in stretch assignments. Often, these projects require working with new teams or departments, providing an excellent opportunity to build relationships and expand your professional network. Collaborating effectively across different functions can enhance your teamwork and communication skills, further contributing to your professional development.

Taking on stretch assignments demonstrates your commitment to your organization's success. It shows that you are invested in the company's goals and are willing to take on challenging tasks to drive progress. This proactive attitude can set you apart as a dedicated and ambitious employee, enhancing your reputation and influence within the organization.

Stretch assignments are a powerful tool for career development. They push you beyond your current capabilities, enabling you to develop new skills, gain valuable experience, and demonstrate your potential to senior management. By approaching these assignments strategically, seeking feedback, and collaborating effectively, you can maximize their benefits and significantly impact your career trajectory. Embracing stretch assignments accelerates your professional growth and positions you as a versatile, committed professional ready to take on more significant challenges and opportunities.

Networking and building relationships are essential components of career advancement. For many, networking does not come naturally, but it is a skill that can be developed and refined. Expanding your network is crucial because it opens doors to new opportunities, mentorship, and collaborations, which are critical professional growth drivers.

First, consider your current networking skills. Are you actively meeting new people and maintaining connections? Effective networking goes beyond simply collecting business cards; it involves building genuine, meaningful relationships. Start by engaging with colleagues from different departments within your company. This internal networking helps you understand various facets of the organization and can lead to collaborative opportunities that enhance your visibility and influence.

Attending industry events is another powerful way to expand your network. Conferences, seminars, and workshops provide platforms to meet professionals who share your interests and goals. These events are opportunities to learn about industry trends, exchange ideas, and establish connections with peers and leaders in your field. When attending these events, be proactive in introducing yourself and participating in discussions. Follow up with the people you meet to maintain the connection and explore potential collaborations.

Engaging with professionals on platforms like LinkedIn is also vital. LinkedIn lets you connect with a vast network of professionals worldwide, share your achievements, and stay updated on industry news. Regularly updating your profile, sharing relevant content, and participating in groups can significantly enhance your online presence. Personalized messages can make your outreach more effective and meaningful when connecting with new contacts.

Building relationships requires more than initial contact; it involves ongoing communication and support. Be genuinely interested in the people you connect with and look for ways to offer them value. This could be through sharing resources, introductions, or helping with their projects. Being helpful and supportive strengthens your professional relationships and creates a network of allies more likely to support you in return.

Mentorship is a significant benefit of networking. Having mentors can provide you with valuable guidance, advice, and support as you navigate your career. Seek mentors within and outside your organization with the experience and knowledge you aspire to gain. A mentor can offer insights into industry trends, help you identify growth opportunities, and provide feedback on your career plans. Building a solid relationship with a mentor involves regular communication, respect for their time, and a willingness to learn.

Collaborations are another advantage of a robust network. Working with professionals from different backgrounds and with varying levels of expertise can lead to innovative solutions and new business opportunities. Collaborative projects can enhance your skills, expand your knowledge, and increase your visibility within the industry. Networking facilitates these collaborations by connecting you with people with complementary skills and interests.

For those who find networking challenging, start small and gradually expand your efforts. Begin by attending local events or joining professional organizations where you can meet like-minded individuals in a more comfortable setting. Practice your networking skills by setting small goals, such as meeting a certain number of new people at each event or reaching out to a new contact each week.

Remember, networking is a two-way street. It is about what others can do for you and what you can offer them. By approaching networking with a genuine desire to build mutually beneficial relationships, you can create a strong, supportive professional network that will be invaluable throughout your career.

Networking and building relationships are critical for career advancement. By actively meeting new people, attending industry events, engaging on platforms like LinkedIn, and maintaining meaningful connections, you can expand your network and open doors to new opportunities, mentorship, and collaborations. Developing networking skills and building genuine relationships will significantly impact your professional growth and success.

Follow these practical steps to make meaningful change happen, ensure you do things differently and effectively drive change.

Start by clearly defining your goal - setting specific, measurable goals. Vague goals like "I want a promotion" do not provide a clear direction. Instead, set specific and measurable targets. For example, aim for "I want to become a senior manager within the next two years by completing a leadership development program and leading a high-impact project. This approach gives you a concrete objective and timeframe, making tracking your progress and staying focused easier.

Develop a detailed plan outlining the steps needed to achieve your goals. This plan should include timelines, resources required, and potential obstacles you might encounter. A well-thought-out plan acts as a roadmap, guiding you through the necessary actions and helping you anticipate challenges. For instance, if your goal is to start a consulting business, your plan might include market research, developing a business plan, building a professional website, and attending networking events.

Regularly seek feedback from peers, mentors, and

supervisors. Constructive feedback is invaluable as it provides insights into areas where you need improvement and helps you stay on track. Actively asking for feedback shows your commitment to growth and willingness to learn from others. Implementing this feedback can refine your approach and ensure you are moving in the right direction.

Keep track of your progress and adjust as needed. It is crucial to regularly review your goals and assess whether your actions are moving you closer to achieving them. This ongoing evaluation allows you to identify what is working and what is not, enabling you to make informed decisions and stay aligned with your objectives.

To illustrate the importance of doing things differently, let us explore a few real-world examples or scenarios.

To start your own consulting business, research the market to identify your niche. Develop a comprehensive business plan that outlines your services, target market, and financial projections. Build a professional website showcasing your expertise and create content that adds value to your potential clients—attending networking events to build relationships with potential clients and industry influencers. This proactive approach not only establishes your presence in the market but also helps you gain valuable insights and connections.

If you aim for a job promotion, take on additional responsibilities demonstrating your leadership potential. Volunteer for cross-functional projects, mentor junior colleagues and continuously improve your skills through training and development programs. Show initiative by identifying areas where you can contribute beyond your current role and consistently deliver high-quality work. This proves your readiness for the next level and highlights your commitment to the organization's success.

To learn a new skill, such as coding or digital marketing, dedicate weekly time to study and practice. Take online courses, join relevant online communities, and work on real-life projects to apply your knowledge. Consistently improving your skills increases your value to your current employer and enhances future career opportunities. By setting aside regular time for learning and applying new knowledge, you can steadily build expertise in the new skill area.

Change can be daunting, and it is natural to encounter resistance. Here are some strategies to overcome this resistance. First, embrace a growth mindset.

Cultivate a mindset that views challenges as opportunities for growth. Believe in your ability to learn and adapt, and see setbacks as part of the learning process. This positive attitude towards change makes it easier to embrace new experiences and persist through difficulties.

It would be best if you started small. Begin with small, manageable changes that can build momentum. Gradually increase the scope and scale of your efforts as you become more comfortable with the process. Small wins can build confidence and demonstrate the benefits of change, making it easier to tackle more considerable challenges over time.

Remember to seek support. Surround yourself with a supportive network of mentors, colleagues, and friends who encourage and motivate you. Their support can provide the confidence and accountability needed to stay committed to your goals. A robust support system can help you navigate challenges and focus on your objectives.

Finally, stay resilient. Understand that change is often accompanied by obstacles and setbacks. Stay resilient, remain focused on your long-term goals, and be prepared to adjust your approach as needed. Resilience is critical to overcoming challenges and maintaining progress towards your goals.

Achieving different results requires doing things differently. By setting clear goals, continuously learning, taking on new challenges, and expanding your network, you position yourself for growth and success. Embrace change, overcome resistance, and stay committed to your journey. Remember, the path to achieving your goals is paved with the willingness to step out of your comfort zone and do things differently.

6

JUST TAKE A STEP FORWARD

Life is full of uncertainties and crossroads. In both your personal and professional journey, you often face moments where the path ahead is unclear. Taking the first step becomes crucial in these moments, even without knowing the exact direction. This chapter discusses the importance of action and how taking that first step can catalyze change and progress.

The Power of Action. The fear of making the wrong choice can be paralyzing. However, there are no wrong steps; every action teaches something valuable. By doing something, you initiate change and begin moving forward. If you do not take that first step, you risk getting stuck and never progressing.

It would be best to embrace uncertainty because uncertainty is a natural part of life. Instead of waiting for the perfect moment or plan, embrace the unknown and act. Here is why:

Learning Through Action: Each step you take provides invaluable lessons, whether it leads to success or failure. These lessons help you refine your approach and make better decisions in the future. Action breeds experience and experience is the best teacher.

Learning through action is a powerful and essential personal and professional growth approach. Each step you take, whether it leads to success or failure, provides invaluable lessons that contribute to your development. These lessons help refine your strategy and enable you to make better decisions in the future. Action breeds experience, and experience, in turn, becomes the best teacher.

When you engage in new activities or take on challenging tasks, you enter a dynamic learning environment where theoretical knowledge meets practical application. This hands-on experience is often more impactful than passive learning methods, such as reading or attending lectures. Through action, you encounter real-world problems and develop practical solutions, which deepen your understanding and hone your skills.

One of the key benefits of learning through action is the immediate feedback it provides. You can quickly see what works and what does not as you act. This real-time feedback allows you to adjust your strategies and methods promptly. For example, if you are leading a project and encounter an unexpected obstacle, you must think on your feet and find a way to overcome it. This process teaches you problem-solving skills and enhances your ability to adapt to changing circumstances.

Failures and setbacks are an inevitable part of acting but are also some of the most valuable learning opportunities. When you experience failure, it forces you to analyze what went wrong and why. This reflection helps you identify areas for improvement and develop more effective approaches for the future. For instance, if a marketing campaign you launched did not achieve the desired results, a thorough analysis might reveal gaps in your strategy or execution. This insight can inform your next campaign, increasing the likelihood of success.

Success achieved through action reinforces effective

behaviors and strategies. Seeing positive outcomes from your efforts builds confidence and motivates you to continue taking proactive steps. Success validates your approach and encourages you to replicate and build upon it in future endeavors. For example, if a new sales technique leads to increased conversions, you can refine and expand this technique, applying it more broadly to achieve even more excellent results.

Learning through action also fosters a growth mindset. It encourages you to view challenges as opportunities for development rather than obstacles. This mindset is crucial for continuous improvement and long-term success. By embracing action as a learning tool, you become more resilient and better equipped to handle uncertainty and change.

Additionally, action-oriented learning promotes creativity and innovation. It would be best if you often thought creatively to solve problems and achieve your goals when you act. This creative problem-solving process can lead to innovative ideas and solutions you might not have discovered through passive learning methods. For example, actively engaging in prototyping and testing can reveal unique features or improvements that theoretical planning alone would not uncover when developing a new product.

Learning through action can also enhance your leadership and teamwork skills in professional settings. Leading projects, making decisions, and collaborating with others in real-world scenarios help you develop practical leadership abilities and strengthen your interpersonal skills. These experiences are invaluable for building trust, fostering collaboration, and driving team success.

It is essential to adopt a reflective practice to maximize the benefits of learning through action. After acting, take the time to reflect on what you did, what the outcomes were, and what you learned from the experience. This reflection can be formal, such as through journaling or structured feedback sessions, or informal, through discussions with colleagues or mentors. The goal is to continuously learn from your actions and apply these lessons to future endeavors.

Learning through action is a powerful method for personal and professional growth. Whether successful or not, each step you take provides invaluable lessons that help refine your approach and improve your decision-making. Action breeds experience and experience is the best teacher. By embracing this approach, you can enhance your skills, foster a growth mindset, and drive continuous improvement and innovation in your career.

Building Momentum: The most challenging part of any journey is often the beginning. By taking the first step, you build momentum. This momentum makes it easier to take the next step and the one after. Progress, no matter how small, fuels motivation and drives you forward.

Building momentum is crucial for overcoming the initial inertia that often accompanies the beginning of any journey. The hardest part is frequently just starting, but once you take the first step, you create a sense of movement that can propel you forward. This momentum is vital because it makes subsequent steps easier, leading to sustained progress and achievement.

Taking the first step, no matter how small, sets a series of actions in motion. It signals a commitment to your goals and breaks the cycle of procrastination and hesitation. For example, if you aim to write a book, the first step might be outlining the chapters or writing the first paragraph. This initial action, however small, reduces the psychological barrier of starting and lays the groundwork for further progress.

Momentum is like a snowball effect. When you start with small, manageable tasks, completing each task builds confidence and motivation. These small wins create a positive feedback loop, encouraging you to continue and tackle more significant challenges. No matter how incremental, each step forward builds on the last, making the overall journey less daunting and more achievable.

Momentum helps maintain focus and consistency. Once you move forward, staying engaged and dedicated to your tasks becomes more accessible. Consistency is critical to success in any endeavor, and momentum ensures you keep moving, even when faced with obstacles. For instance, daily practice gradually builds your skills if you are learning a new language. Missing a day or two can disrupt this momentum, but maintaining a consistent schedule reinforces learning and leads to steady improvement.

Progress, even in small increments, fuels motivation and drives you forward. Seeing tangible results, however minor, can significantly boost your morale and reinforce your commitment to your goals. This is why breaking larger tasks into smaller, actionable steps is practical. Each completed step is a milestone, providing a sense of accomplishment and motivating you to keep going.

Momentum also plays a crucial role in overcoming setbacks. When you build momentum, a temporary setback is less likely to derail your progress. The forward motion you have created makes it easier to bounce back and continue moving towards your objectives. For example, if you are training for a marathon and miss a few days due to illness, the momentum built from your previous training makes it easier to resume your routine and regain your pace.

Setting clear, achievable goals and creating a structured action plan are essential to building and sustaining momentum. Start with easy tasks and gradually increase their complexity as you build confidence and capability. Celebrate small victories along the way to reinforce positive behavior and maintain motivation.

Accountability is another powerful tool for building momentum. Sharing your goals with a mentor, coach, or supportive peers can encourage and hold you accountable for your progress. Regular check-ins and feedback can help keep you on track and committed to your journey.

Maintaining a positive mindset is critical. Acknowledge

that the beginning is often the most challenging part and that every step, no matter how small, is a step towards your goal. Visualize your success and remind yourself of the reasons behind your goals. This mental reinforcement can help sustain your drive and determination.

Building momentum is essential for overcoming the initial challenges of any journey. Taking the first step and creating a sense of movement makes it easier to take subsequent steps and maintain progress. This momentum fuels motivation, builds confidence, and drives you forward, making achieving your goals through consistent, incremental actions possible. Embrace the power of small wins, maintain focus and consistency, and leverage accountability and a positive mindset to sustain momentum and propel yourself toward success.

Overcoming Fear: Fear of failure or making mistakes can be a significant barrier. By acting, you confront and overcome this fear. Whatever the outcome, each step you take builds your confidence and resilience.

Overcoming fear is a critical aspect of personal and professional growth. Fear of failure or making mistakes can be a significant barrier, often preventing us from taking the necessary steps to achieve our goals. However, by acting despite these fears, we confront and gradually overcome them. Each step you take, regardless of the outcome, builds your confidence and resilience, enabling you to tackle even more significant challenges in the future.

Fear of failure is a common obstacle that paralyzes action and stifles progress. It is natural to worry about the potential adverse outcomes of our actions, but it is essential to recognize that failure is an inherent part of the learning process. Instead of viewing failure as a reflection of your abilities, see it as a valuable opportunity to learn and grow. Every mistake provides insights into what does not work, guiding you toward better strategies and solutions.

Even when you feel fearful, acting is the most effective way to diminish that fear. Doing something, no matter how small, breaks the cycle of inaction and hesitation. For instance, if you are afraid of public speaking, starting with small presentations to a few colleagues can help you gradually build confidence. Each successful experience, no matter how minor, reinforces your belief in your ability to handle similar situations in the future.

You build resilience when confronting your fears and

taking steps towards your goals. Resilience is the ability to bounce back from setbacks and progress despite challenges. This trait is crucial for long-term success, as it allows you to maintain your momentum and motivation even when things do not go as planned. By repeatedly facing and overcoming your fears, you develop a mental toughness that equips you to handle adversity with grace and determination.

Acting in the face of fear helps you develop a growth mindset. A growth mindset is the belief that your abilities and intelligence can be developed through dedication and hard work. This perspective encourages you to embrace challenges, persist through difficulties, and view effort as a path to mastery. Adopting a growth mindset makes you more likely to take risks and seize opportunities, knowing that each successful experience contributes to your personal development.

It is also important to reframe your perception of fear. Instead of seeing fear as a signal to stop, view it as a sign that you are stepping out of your comfort zone and into a space where growth occurs. Fear often indicates that you are on the verge of something significant, pushing you towards new achievements and possibilities. Embrace this discomfort as a necessary part of the journey towards your goals.

One practical strategy for overcoming fear is to break down your goals into smaller, more manageable tasks. This approach reduces the overwhelming nature of significant goals and makes it easier to take the first step. Each small success builds your confidence and makes the next step less daunting. For example, if you want to start a new business but fear the risks involved, begin by researching your market, creating a business plan, and seeking advice from experienced entrepreneurs. These smaller steps are less intimidating and help you build the confidence to launch your venture.

Additionally, seeking support from mentors, peers, or professional networks can provide valuable encouragement and guidance. Sharing your fears with others can alleviate some pressure and help you gain different perspectives on addressing them. Mentors and supportive colleagues can offer practical advice, share their experiences of overcoming fear, and provide reassurance that setbacks are a normal part of the process.

Overcoming fear requires action and a shift in mindset. You build confidence and resilience by confronting your fears and taking steps towards your goals. Embrace failure as a learning opportunity, develop a growth mindset, and view fear as a sign of growth. Break down your goals into manageable tasks and seek support from others. Regardless of the outcome, each step contributes to your development and brings you closer to achieving your aspirations.

What are the practical steps to move forward? To start, set small, achievable goals. Start with small, manageable goals that are easy to achieve. These small wins build confidence and encourage further action. Break down your larger objectives into smaller tasks and focus on completing them one at a time.

It would be best if you adopted a growth mindset. Embrace a perspective that views challenges and setbacks as opportunities for growth. Understand that every step, even if it does not lead to immediate success, contributes to your overall development.

I cannot say this enough: you need to seek feedback. As you take steps forward, seek feedback from others. Constructive feedback can provide guidance, highlight areas for improvement, and help you adjust your course effectively.

Another critical aspect is to reflect and adjust; do not be rigid. Regularly take time to reflect on your progress. Assess what is working and what is not, and be willing to adapt your approach as needed. Flexibility and adaptability are crucial to navigating an uncertain path.

To illustrate the concept of taking steps forward, let us explore a few scenarios:

Career Transition: If you are considering a career change but are unsure of the exact direction, start by exploring new fields. Attend industry events, take online courses, and connect with professionals in those areas. Each step, such as enrolling in a class or conducting an informational interview, brings you closer to discovering the right path.

Starting a Business: If you dream of starting your own business but feel overwhelmed by the magnitude of the task, begin with small steps. Write a business plan, research your market, and network with potential customers or mentors. Each action, no matter how small, contributes to building your business.

Skill Development: If you want to learn a new skill but are unsure where to start, enroll in a course or set aside time each day for practice. The initial step might be challenging, but it will put you on a path of continuous improvement and growth.

However, persistence is essential. Taking a step forward is just the beginning. Persistence and perseverance are critical to maintaining progress. There will be times when you face obstacles and setbacks, but it is crucial to keep moving. Progress is not always linear, and setbacks are part of the journey.

The most crucial step in the journey of life is the first one. By taking that initial step, you break free from inertia and start moving toward your goals. Embrace uncertainty, learn from your actions, and keep moving forward. There are no wrong steps, only lessons that guide you toward success.

Take a step forward today. It might be small and uncertain, but it is the beginning of change and progress. Keep stepping, learning, and moving toward the future you envision.

7

MANIFEST YOUR OUTCOMES

Making your dreams come true is not just wishful thinking; it is about focused action, desire, and unwavering determination. This chapter will explore how to manifest your outcomes by concentrating on the actions and decisions that directly contribute to your goals. Everything else should become secondary.

Understanding the power of focus is critical to manifesting your outcomes; you must focus on the actions and decisions that bring you closer to your desired goals. This requires a laser-sharp focus on what truly matters. Here is how to harness the power of focus:

Setting clear goals is a fundamental step in manifesting

your outcomes. When you precisely define what you want to achieve, it becomes much easier to map out the steps needed. Your goals should adhere to the SMART criteria: Specific, Measurable, Achievable, Relevant, and Time-bound. This structured approach ensures that your goals are clear and actionable, laying the groundwork for successful outcomes.

Clearly define what you want to achieve. Your goals should be specific, measurable, achievable, relevant, and time-bound (SMART). When you know precisely what you wish to do, mapping out the steps needed to get there becomes more accessible.

Measurable goals allow you to track your progress and determine when you have achieved them. Incorporate concrete criteria to evaluate your progress. For instance, if your goal is to improve your sales performance, you might set a measurable goal like "I want to increase my sales by 20% over the next six months." This measurability provides a clear benchmark against which you can measure your success.

Achievable goals are realistic and attainable, given your current resources and constraints. Setting overly ambitious goals can lead to frustration and demotivation if they are not realistically attainable. Assess your situation and ensure that your goals are challenging yet feasible. For example, aiming to double your monthly income might not be realistic, but setting a goal to increase it by 10% over a year might be more achievable.

Relevant goals align with your broader objectives and values. They should be meaningful and contribute to your long-term vision. For instance, if you value work-life balance, setting a goal to work 80 hours a week might not be relevant to your overall well-being. Instead, an appropriate goal could be "I want to increase my efficiency at work so that I can leave the office by 6 PM every day." This ensures that your goals are aligned with your personal and professional aspirations.

Time-bound goals have a clear deadline, creating a sense of urgency and helping you prioritize your efforts. A deadline motivates you to act and prevents procrastination. For example, instead of saying, "I want to write a book someday," set a time-bound goal like "I want to complete the first draft of my book by December 31st." This time constraint encourages consistent progress and helps you stay focused.

Once your goals are set, it becomes easier to map out the steps needed to achieve them. Break down each goal into smaller, actionable tasks. This step-by-step approach makes significant goals more manageable and less overwhelming. For instance, if your goal is to become a senior project manager, your steps might include completing a relevant certification, seeking mentorship from current senior managers, and taking on more complex projects to build your experience.

As you work towards your goals, be prepared to adjust and adapt your plan as needed. Unexpected challenges and opportunities may arise, requiring flexibility in your approach. Regularly review your progress and make necessary adjustments to stay on track. This adaptive mindset ensures that you remain resilient and responsive to changes, increasing your likelihood of success.

Enlist the support of mentors, colleagues, or friends who can provide guidance and hold you accountable. Sharing your goals with others increases your commitment and creates a support network to help you stay on track. Regular check-ins with an accountability partner can provide valuable feedback and encouragement, keeping you motivated and focused.

Setting clear goals using the SMART criteria is essential for manifesting your outcomes. Specific, measurable, achievable, relevant, and time-bound goals provide a clear roadmap for success. You create a structured and actionable plan by mapping the steps needed to achieve your goals, visualizing your success, and seeking support. This approach clarifies your path forward and enhances your motivation and commitment, bringing you closer to achieving your aspirations.

Nex is to focus on prioritizing your tasks. Not all tasks are created equally. Identify the functions that impact your goals most and prioritize them. Use tools like the Eisenhower Matrix to categorize tasks by urgency and importance, ensuring that your focus remains on high-impact activities.

Prioritizing your tasks is essential for effective goal achievement. Not all tasks are created equal; some have a far more significant impact on your goals than others. By identifying and focusing on these high-impact activities, you can ensure that your efforts are directed toward what truly matters. Tools like the Eisenhower Matrix can help you categorize tasks by urgency and importance, keeping your focus on the most critical activities.

The Eisenhower Matrix, or the Urgent-Important Matrix, is a powerful tool for task prioritization. It divides tasks into four categories based on their urgency and importance:

1. **Urgent and Important:** These tasks require immediate attention and are critical to achieving your goals. They often involve deadlines or crises that need prompt resolution. Prioritize these tasks first to prevent any negative consequences from delays.
2. **Important but Not Urgent:** These tasks are crucial for long-term success but do not require immediate action. They include activities like strategic planning, skill development, and relationship building—schedule time for these tasks to ensure steady progress toward your goals.
3. **Urgent but Not Important:** These tasks demand immediate attention but do not significantly contribute to your long-term objectives. They often include interruptions, meetings, and minor issues. Delegate these

tasks if possible or manage them efficiently to minimize their impact on your time.

4. **Not Urgent and Not Important:** These tasks have little to no impact on your goals and can often be considered distractions. Limit the time spent on these activities or eliminate them to free up time for more critical tasks.

To prioritize effectively, start by identifying the tasks that most impact your goals. These activities directly contribute to your key objectives and drive meaningful progress. For example, suppose your goal is to advance in your career. In that case, high-impact tasks might include completing a professional certification, networking with industry leaders, and leading high-visibility projects at work.

You are focusing on High-Impact Activities. Once you have identified your high-impact tasks, allocate your time and resources accordingly. Dedicate most of your efforts to these activities, ensuring they receive the attention and energy they deserve. This focused approach prevents you from getting sidetracked by less important tasks and maximizes productivity.

It would be best if you used the Eisenhower Matrix. Implementing the Eisenhower Matrix involves regularly reviewing and categorizing your tasks. Start by listing all the tasks you need to complete. Then, categorize each task into one of the four quadrants of the matrix. This visual representation helps you quickly identify where to focus your efforts. Review and update your matrix frequently to adapt to changing priorities and demands.

As with everything in life, you need balance, and creating a balanced schedule is critical.

A well-balanced schedule incorporates time for both urgent and essential tasks. Allocate specific blocks of time for high-priority activities, ensuring that less critical tasks do not overshadow them. For example, dedicate your most productive hours to essential but not urgent tasks, such as strategic planning or skill development. Reserve time for urgent and important tasks as they arise and manage urgent but not important tasks efficiently.

Eliminating distractions is hard. Distractions can significantly hinder your productivity and derail your progress toward your goals. Identify common distractions in your work environment and develop strategies to minimize them. This might involve setting boundaries with colleagues, turning off non-essential notifications, or creating a dedicated workspace. By reducing distractions, you can maintain focus on your high-impact tasks.

I am leveraging technology and tools to help with this. Numerous tools and technologies help you prioritize and manage your tasks. Project management software, task management apps, and calendar tools can streamline your workflow and keep you organized. Use these tools to set deadlines, track progress, and remind yourself of upcoming tasks. Technology can enhance efficiency and ensure you stay on top of your priorities.

Remember to review and adjust priorities regularly. Priorities can change, so reviewing and adjusting your task list is essential. Set aside time each week to evaluate your progress and reassess your priorities. This ongoing review process ensures that you remain aligned with your goals and can adapt to new challenges or opportunities.

But it would be best if you stayed disciplined and committed. Prioritizing tasks requires discipline and commitment. Getting caught up in day-to-day activities and losing sight of your high-impact goals is easy. Stay committed to your priorities by reminding yourself of the bigger picture and the long-term benefits of your efforts.

Consistent focus and dedication will yield meaningful results over time.

Prioritizing your tasks is crucial for manifesting your outcomes. By identifying high-impact activities, using tools like the Eisenhower Matrix, and staying disciplined, you can ensure that your focus remains on what truly matters. This strategic approach to task management enhances productivity, drives meaningful progress, and brings you closer to achieving your goals.

Your next challenge is to eliminate distractions that can derail your progress. Identify what distracts you and take steps to minimize or eliminate it. This could mean setting boundaries, creating a focused workspace, or using tools to block distracting websites.

You cannot have focus without the role of desire – you must want it and want it badly.

Eliminating distractions is crucial for maintaining focus and ensuring steady progress toward your goals. Distractions can significantly derail your efforts, wasting time and decreased productivity. By identifying what distracts you and taking proactive steps to minimize or eliminate these distractions, you can create an environment conducive to achieving your objectives.

The first step in eliminating distractions is to identify them. Take note of the things that often pull your attention away from your work. These could be external distractions, such as noisy environments, interruptions from colleagues, social media notifications, or internal distractions, like procrastination, stress, or fatigue. Understanding what distracts you is essential for developing effective strategies to address them.

Setting boundaries is a powerful way to minimize distractions. Communicate your focused time needs to colleagues, friends, and family members. Let them know when you are unavailable for interruptions and ask for their cooperation in respecting your work time. For example, you could establish "do not disturb" hours while focusing solely on high-priority tasks. This transparent communication helps create an environment where you can work uninterrupted.

I find it helpful when I create a focused workspace; a dedicated workspace can significantly enhance your ability to concentrate. Designate a specific area for work that is free from everyday distractions. Ensure this space is organized and equipped with everything you need to work efficiently. A clean and tidy workspace reduces visual clutter, which can be a source of distraction. Personalize your workspace to make it comfortable and inspiring, boosting your motivation and focus.

Again, I use tools and technology to block distractions. Technology can be both a source of distraction and a solution for it. Utilize tools and apps to block distracting websites and apps during work hours. For example, applications like Freedom, Cold Turkey, or StayFocusd can restrict access to social media, news sites, and other online distractions. These tools help you stay focused on your tasks by eliminating the temptation to browse unrelated content.

Implement time management techniques. Effective time management techniques can help you stay focused and productive. Techniques such as the Pomodoro Technique, where you work for a set period (typically 25 minutes) followed by a short break, can enhance concentration and prevent burnout. This structured approach to work and rest helps maintain elevated levels of focus and productivity throughout the day.

Digital distractions like email notifications, instant messages, and social media alerts can constantly interrupt your workflow. Take control of these distractions by turning off non-essential notifications during work hours. Set specific times to check and respond to emails and messages rather than allowing them to disrupt your focus continually. Use productivity tools like email filters and task management apps to organize and prioritize digital communications.

It would be best if you managed internal distractions. Internal distractions, such as stress, anxiety, and fatigue, can be just as disruptive as external ones. Address these by incorporating stress management and self-care practices into your routine. Regular exercise, mindfulness meditation, and adequate sleep are essential for maintaining mental clarity and focus. Additionally, break large tasks into smaller, manageable steps to prevent feeling overwhelmed, and take regular breaks to recharge.

Establish good routines and habits. Developing consistent routines and habits can create a structured environment that minimizes distractions. Establish a daily schedule with dedicated time blocks for focused work, breaks, and other activities. Consistency in your routine helps train your mind to switch into work mode during designated times, making it easier to concentrate and stay productive.

Multitasking is a myth, and you need to limit multitasking. Multitasking can dilute your focus and reduce overall productivity. Instead of juggling multiple tasks simultaneously, practice single-tasking by focusing on one task at a time. This approach allows you to give your full attention to each task, improving the quality of your work and reducing the likelihood of errors. Prioritize your tasks and tackle them sequentially to maintain an elevated level of focus and efficiency.

One way to do this is to seek accountability. Having someone hold you accountable can help you stay on track and minimize distractions. Share your goals and progress with a mentor, coach, or accountability partner who can provide support and encouragement. Regular check-ins and progress reviews create a sense of responsibility and motivate you to stay focused and committed to your tasks.

Eliminating distractions is vital for maintaining focus and achieving your goals. By identifying your distractions, setting boundaries, creating a focused workspace, and using tools to block digital interruptions, you can create an environment conducive to productivity. Implement time management techniques, manage internal distractions, establish consistent routines, limit multitasking, and seek accountability to enhance your focus and drive steady progress toward your objectives.

Desire is the fuel that drives your actions. A burning desire to achieve your goals will keep you motivated even when the going gets tough. Here is how to cultivate and maintain your desire:

Regularly visualize your success. Imagine yourself achieving your goals and their positive impact on your life. Visualization can reinforce your desire and keep you motivated.

Visualization is a powerful tool for manifesting your outcomes. Spend time visualizing your success and imagining the steps you need to take to achieve it. This mental rehearsal helps reinforce your commitment and prepares you for the challenges ahead. Visualizing your goals can boost your motivation and keep you focused on your desired outcomes.

Stay Passionate: Engage in activities that reignite your passion for your goals. This could be reading success stories, attending motivational seminars, or connecting with like-minded individuals. Passion sustains your desire and keeps you committed.

Set Milestones: Break your larger goals into smaller,

manageable milestones. Celebrating these small victories can keep your desire burning and provide a sense of accomplishment.

You cannot underestimate the importance of determination and the role it plays. Determination is the unwavering commitment to achieving your goals despite challenges and setbacks. It is about pushing through obstacles and maintaining a steadfast resolve. Here is how to cultivate determination:

Develop Resilience: Understand that setbacks are a part of any journey. Develop a resilient mindset that views challenges as opportunities to learn and grow. Resilience helps you bounce back stronger from failures.

Maintain Consistency: Consistency is critical to progress. Create a routine or schedule that incorporates regular actions toward your goals. Even small, consistent efforts can lead to meaningful results over time.

Seek Accountability: Find someone to hold you accountable for your actions. This could be a mentor, a coach, or a peer group. Accountability ensures that you stay on track and committed to your goals.

What practical steps can you take to manifest your outcomes? Here are some ideas:

Create a Vision Board: A vision board is a powerful tool for visually representing your goals and dreams. Place it somewhere you will see it daily. It will constantly remind you of what you are working towards and help keep your focus sharp.

Develop an Action Plan: Outline the specific actions you need to take to achieve your goals. This plan should include timelines, resources needed, and potential obstacles. An action plan provides a clear roadmap and helps you stay organized.

Monitor Your Progress: Regularly review your progress towards your goals. This allows you to make necessary adjustments and ensures you are on the right track. Use tools like journals or apps to track your progress and reflect on your journey.

To illustrate the concept of manifesting your outcomes, let us consider a few scenarios:

Career Advancement: If your goal is to advance, focus on acquiring the skills and experiences to make you a strong candidate for promotion. This might involve further education, taking on leadership roles, or seeking mentorship. Stay determined, visualize your success, and take consistent action.

Entrepreneurship: If you dream of starting your own business, prioritize actions that move you closer to this goal. Develop a business plan, conduct market research, and build a network of potential clients and partners. Maintain a strong desire for success and remain determined through the inevitable challenges.

Personal Development: If your goal is personal growth, focus on activities contributing to your development. These could include reading, attending workshops, or practicing new skills. Stay passionate about your growth and remain consistent in your efforts.

Manifesting your outcomes is all about focus, desire, and determination. You can make your dreams a reality by setting clear goals, prioritizing impactful tasks, and maintaining a strong passion and unwavering determination. Everything else should become secondary as you channel your energy towards the actions that directly contribute to your success.

The power to manifest your outcomes lies within you. Stay focused, stay passionate, and stay determined. The journey may be challenging, but the rewards are worth the effort. Keep your eyes on your goals, take consistent action, and watch your dreams become reality.

8

IGNORE THE NOISE

Today, more than ever, distractions are everywhere. From social media notifications to unsolicited advice, it is easy to get sidetracked and lose focus on what truly matters. This chapter concerns cutting through the noise and staying laser-focused on your goals. You can maintain clarity, productivity, and progress toward your desired outcomes by ignoring distractions.

The first thing to do is to understand the noise because recognizing it makes it easier to ignore. Noise, in this context, refers to anything that diverts your attention from your primary goals. This can include:

We all know and have digital distractions, such as

emails, social media, and constant notifications, interrupting our workflow.

Digital distractions are a significant hindrance to productivity and focus. Emails, social media, and constant notifications can continuously interrupt your workflow, making it challenging to maintain concentration and achieve your goals. Understanding how to manage and minimize these distractions is crucial for creating an environment conducive to sustained productivity.

Emails are a necessary part of professional communication but can also be distracting. Constant email notifications can divert attention from important tasks, disrupting workflow and reducing efficiency. Here are some strategies to manage email distractions:

Schedule Specific Times for Email: Instead of checking your email constantly throughout the day, designate specific times to read and respond to emails. For example, you might check your email first thing in the morning, after lunch, and at the end of the day. This approach helps you stay focused on your tasks without frequent interruptions.

Use Email Filters and Folders: Organize your inbox with filters and folders to prioritize essential emails and manage less critical ones. Automatically direct newsletters, promotional emails, and other non-urgent messages to specific folders, allowing you to focus on high-priority emails first.

Turn Off Notifications: Disable email notifications on your computer and mobile devices to prevent constant interruptions. This allows you to control when you check your email rather than being dictated by incoming messages.

Set Expectations: Communicate with your colleagues and clients about your email response times. Let them know that you check and respond to emails at specific times, which can help manage their expectations and reduce the pressure to respond immediately.

Social media platforms are designed to capture your attention and keep you engaged, often leading to prolonged periods of distraction. Here is how to manage social media distractions effectively:

Limit Social Media Use: Set specific times for checking social media, such as during your lunch break or after work hours. Avoid logging into social media accounts during peak productivity periods.

Use Browser Extensions: Install browser extensions

like StayFocusd, Freedom, or Cold Turkey that block access to social media sites during designated work hours. These tools can help you resist the temptation to check social media frequently.

Log Out of Accounts: Logging out of your social media accounts can create an extra barrier to accessing these platforms. This simple step can deter you from mindlessly scrolling through your feeds when you should be focusing on work.

Unfollow and Mute: Reduce the noise in your social media feeds by unfollowing or muting accounts that post distracting content. Curate your feed to include only valuable, relevant information contributing to your personal or professional growth.

Notifications are the bane of my existence. Constant notifications from various apps and devices can fragment your attention and make it challenging to stay on task. Here is how to manage notifications effectively:

Customize Notification Settings: Review your device's notification settings and turn off non-essential notifications. Prioritize critical notifications and silence those that are not immediately relevant.

Use Do Not Disturb Mode: During work hours,

activate the "Do Not Disturb" mode on your devices to block incoming notifications. This feature can help you maintain a focused work environment without interruptions.

Set Notification Priorities: Some devices and apps allow you to set notification priorities. Configure these settings to ensure that only the most critical alerts get through while others are muted or delayed.

Batch Process Notifications: Instead of addressing notifications as they come in, set specific times to review and respond to them. This approach prevents constant interruptions and allows you to handle notifications in a more controlled and efficient manner.

Start with creating a focused digital environment. Beyond managing specific digital distractions, it is essential to develop an overall digital environment that supports focus and productivity:

Clean Up Your Digital Workspace: Organize your desktop, files, and applications to reduce digital clutter. A tidy digital workspace can help minimize distractions and make finding the necessary tools and information more accessible.

Use Productivity Tools: Leverage productivity tools

and apps that help you stay organized and focused. Task management apps, digital calendars, and project management software can streamline your workflow and keep you on track.

Set Digital Boundaries: Establish clear boundaries for digital device use. For example, you might decide to keep your phone in another room during work hours or limit personal device use to specific times of the day.

Practice Mindfulness: Incorporate mindfulness practices to stay present and focused. Techniques such as deep breathing, meditation, or short breaks can help you regain focus and reduce the impact of digital distractions.

Digital distractions like emails, social media, and constant notifications can significantly disrupt your workflow and productivity. You can create a more focused and efficient work environment by implementing strategies to manage and minimize these distractions. Schedule specific times for email and social media use, customize notification settings, and leverage productivity tools to maintain concentration and achieve your goals. Taking control of your digital environment can enhance your ability to stay focused and productive in a digitally connected world.

Nothing is worse than unsolicited advice to cause a distraction, especially opinions and suggestions from others that may not align with your vision or goals.

Unsolicited advice can often distract and confuse you, diverting you from your path and undermining your confidence in your own decisions. While opinions and suggestions from others can sometimes be valuable, they may not always align with your vision or goals. It is crucial to manage unsolicited advice effectively to stay focused on your objectives and maintain clarity in your decision-making process.

It is understanding the impact of unsolicited advice. Unsolicited advice, especially when it comes from well-meaning friends, family, or colleagues, can significantly affect your mindset and direction. It can cause self-doubt and make you second-guess your decisions, even if they were based on careful consideration and alignment with your goals. Recognizing the influence of such advice is the first step towards managing it effectively.

It would be best if you stayed true to your vision. Your vision and goals are unique to you and shaped by your experiences, values, and aspirations. While it is essential to be open to new ideas and perspectives, staying true to your vision is equally important. Unsolicited advice may come from individuals who do not fully understand your objectives or the context in which you operate. Trusting your judgment and staying aligned with your vision helps maintain focus and ensures that your actions are purposeful and directed towards your desired outcomes.

When you receive unsolicited advice, consider the source. Ask yourself whether the person offering the advice has the experience, knowledge, and understanding of your situation to provide valuable input. Advice from someone who has successfully navigated similar challenges or has expertise in your field can be worth considering. On the other hand, advice from individuals who lack relevant experience or understanding may not be as helpful and can be disregarded.

Not all advice, even well-intentioned, will be relevant or applicable to your situation. Take the time to assess whether the advice aligns with your goals and whether it can be practically applied. For example, a colleague might suggest a strategy that worked well in their context but may not suit your unique circumstances. Consider the relevance and potential impact of the advice before deciding whether to incorporate it into your plans.

Setting boundaries is essential for managing unsolicited advice. Politely but firmly communicate your need to focus on your goals and vision. Let others know that while you appreciate their input, you have a clear plan and direction to follow. This approach helps minimize unwanted distractions and reinforces your commitment to your objectives.

While unsolicited advice can be distracting, constructive feedback is valuable. Actively seek feedback from trusted mentors, advisors, and peers who have a personal stake in your success and understand your goals. Constructive feedback is usually specific, actionable, and aligned with your objectives, helping you improve and stay on track.

Building confidence in your decision-making abilities is crucial for managing unsolicited advice. Reflect on your past successes and the decisions that led to positive outcomes. Recognize that you have the knowledge and capability to make informed choices that align with your goals. This confidence will help you stay resolute despite conflicting opinions and advice.

Practice Mindfulness. Mindfulness practices can help you stay centered and focused, making it easier to filter out noise and distractions, including unsolicited advice. Meditation, deep breathing, and journaling can enhance your self-awareness and clarity, allowing you to process advice without being overwhelmed. Mindfulness helps you maintain a balanced perspective and stay connected to your vision.

Communicating your vision and goals to others can help you manage unsolicited advice. When people understand your objectives and the rationale behind your decisions, they are more likely to offer relevant and supportive input. Sharing your vision can inspire others to align their suggestions with your goals, making the advice more pertinent and helpful.

Trust your intuition. Your intuition is a powerful guide in decision-making. While it is important to consider external input, trust your instincts when evaluating advice. Your intuition, informed by your experiences and values, often provides valuable insights that align with your true intentions and goals. Trusting your intuition helps you navigate through conflicting advice and stay focused on your path.

Unsolicited advice can be a significant source of distraction and confusion. By staying true to your vision, evaluating the source and relevance of advice, setting boundaries, and seeking constructive feedback; you can manage unsolicited advice effectively. Building confidence in your decisions, practicing mindfulness, communicating your vision, and trusting your intuition are vital strategies for maintaining focus and clarity in the face of external input. By managing unsolicited advice wisely, you can stay aligned with your goals and achieve your desired outcomes.

This leads to negative influences, whether from people or environments, that drain your energy and motivation. Negative influences, whether from people or environments, can drain your energy and motivation, making it challenging to stay focused and productive. These influences can hinder your progress and prevent you from achieving your goals. By effectively identifying and managing negative influences, you can create a more positive and supportive environment that fosters growth and success.

The first step in managing negative influences is to identify them. Negative influences can come from various sources, including toxic relationships, unsupportive colleagues, pessimistic attitudes, and chaotic environments. Reflect on your interactions and surroundings to pinpoint what or who consistently leaves you feeling drained, demotivated, or stressed. Recognizing these influences is crucial for taking action to mitigate their impact.

Once you have identified negative influences, assess their impact on your energy and motivation. Consider how these influences affect your mood, productivity, and overall well-being. For example, a colleague who constantly criticizes your work or an environment filled with constant noise and interruptions can significantly hinder your ability to concentrate and perform at your best. Understanding the extent of the impact helps prioritize which influences to address first.

Setting boundaries is essential for protecting your energy and maintaining a positive mindset. Communicate your limits to those who have a negative influence on you. For instance, if a coworker frequently engages in gossip or negative talk, let them know you prefer to focus on constructive and positive conversations. Establishing boundaries helps create a healthier environment and reduces the time and energy spent on negative interactions.

In some cases, it may be necessary to limit your exposure to negative influences. This could mean reducing the time spent with toxic individuals or avoiding disruptive environments. For example, consider working remotely or finding a quieter workplace space if your workplace environment is chaotic. If a particular relationship consistently brings you down, limit your interactions with that person or seek out more positive and supportive relationships.

Actively seek out positive influences that uplift and motivate you. Surround yourself with people who inspire, support, and encourage you. Positive relationships can provide valuable emotional support, boost confidence, and help you focus on your goals. Additionally, create an environment that fosters positivity by organizing your workspace, adding inspiring elements, and minimizing clutter and distractions.

Cultivating a positive mindset can help you counteract the effects of negative influences. Practice gratitude by regularly reflecting on the things you are thankful for. Focus on your strengths and achievements rather than dwelling on setbacks or criticisms. Engage in positive self-talk to reinforce your confidence and resilience.

Maintaining a positive outlook can help you better manage negative influences and stay motivated.

Prioritizing self-care is essential for maintaining your energy and motivation. Ensure you sleep well, eat a balanced diet, and exercise regularly. Engage in relaxing and rejuvenating activities, such as reading, meditating, or spending time in nature. Taking care of your physical and mental well-being enhances your ability to cope with negative influences and stay focused on your goals.

Sometimes, dealing with negative influences requires external support. Seek guidance from mentors, coaches, or therapists who can provide valuable insights and strategies for managing difficult situations. Supportive relationships can offer a unique perspective and help you develop effective coping mechanisms.

Keeping your goals at the forefront of your mind can help you stay motivated despite negative influences. Regularly remind yourself of your objectives and the reasons behind them. Visualize your success and the positive outcomes of your efforts. This focus can provide the drive and determination needed to overcome obstacles and stay on track.

Building resilience is critical to managing negative

influences. Resilience allows you to bounce back from setbacks and maintain motivation even in adversity. Develop resilience by embracing challenges, learning from failures, and maintaining a growth mindset. The more resilient you become, the less impact negative influences will have on your progress.

Negative influences from people or environments can drain your energy and motivation, hindering your progress. You can create a supportive environment that fosters growth by identifying and assessing these influences, setting boundaries, limiting exposure, and positively surrounding yourself. Developing a positive mindset, practicing self-care, seeking support, focusing on your goals, and building resilience are essential strategies for overcoming negative influences and achieving your desired outcomes.

Stop focusing on irrelevant tasks and activities that do not contribute to your progress but consume your time and resources.

Irrelevant tasks are activities that do not contribute to your progress yet consume your time and resources. These tasks can distract you from your primary goals and impede your productivity. Identifying and minimizing irrelevant tasks is crucial for maintaining focus and ensuring that your efforts are directed toward activities that drive meaningful progress.

The first step in managing irrelevant tasks is to identify them. Reflect on your daily activities and consider which tasks do not align with your goals or contribute to your success. Common examples include excessive email checking, attending unnecessary meetings, engaging in non-productive social media browsing, and performing tasks that could be delegated or automated. By recognizing these time-wasting activities, you can take steps to eliminate or reduce them.

To determine whether a task is relevant, assess its alignment with your goals and objectives. Ask yourself whether the task directly contributes to your progress or is distracting. For example, if your goal is to complete a significant project, spending excessive time organizing your files or tweaking minor details may not be relevant. Prioritize tasks that directly impact your goals and set aside or delegate those that do not.

Again, use the Eisenhower Matrix. The Eisenhower Matrix, or Urgent-Important Matrix, is a valuable tool for categorizing tasks based on their urgency and importance.

You can quickly identify irrelevant tasks by organizing tasks into four quadrants—urgent and important, important but not urgent, urgent but not necessary, and not urgent and not important. Focus on activities in the "important" quadrants and minimize those in the "not important" quadrants.

Delegation and automation are effective strategies for managing irrelevant tasks. Identify tasks that can be delegated to others, such as administrative work or routine tasks that do not require your expertise. Delegating these tasks frees up your time to focus on high-impact activities. Additionally, explore tools and technologies that can automate repetitive tasks like scheduling, data entry, or email management. Automation reduces the burden of manual tasks and enhances efficiency.

Establishing clear priorities helps you stay focused on relevant tasks. Define your top priorities for each day, week, and month, and allocate your time and resources accordingly. Use to-do lists, planners, and project management software to organize and track tasks. By keeping your priorities front and center, you can ensure you spend your time on activities that drive progress.

I bought a desk timer to practice time blocking. Time

blocking is a time management technique that involves scheduling specific blocks of time for focused work on tasks. Dedicating uninterrupted time to high-priority activities can minimize distractions and enhance productivity. Schedule time blocks for your most important tasks and avoid multitasking during these periods. This structured approach helps you stay on track and avoid spending time on irrelevant activities.

Review your tasks and activities regularly to ensure they remain aligned with your goals. Conduct periodic assessments of how you spend your time and identify any irrelevant tasks that have crept into your routine. Adjust your schedule and priorities as needed to maintain focus on what truly matters. Continuous evaluation and adjustment help you stay agile and responsive to changing demands.

Setting boundaries and learning to say no are essential for managing irrelevant tasks. Be assertive in declining tasks and commitments that do not align with your goals. Politely but firmly communicate your priorities to colleagues, friends, and family. Setting clear boundaries can protect your time and energy for activities that contribute to your progress.

Distractions can lead to engaging in irrelevant tasks. Create a focused work environment by minimizing potential distractions. Turn off non-essential notifications, set up a dedicated workspace, and establish a routine that minimizes interruptions. A distraction-free environment allows you to concentrate on high-impact activities and reduces the likelihood of getting sidetracked by irrelevant tasks.

Reflecting on the outcomes of your efforts can help you identify and eliminate irrelevant tasks. Regularly assess the results of your activities and consider whether they contribute to your overall goals. Consider removing certain functions from your routine if they consistently yield little or no value. This reflection process ensures that your efforts are aligned with your desired outcomes and helps you stay focused on what truly matters.

Irrelevant tasks consume time and resources without contributing to your progress. You can prioritize high-impact activities by identifying these tasks, assessing their relevance, and using tools like the Eisenhower Matrix. Delegate and automate where possible, set clear priorities, practice time blocking, and regularly review and adjust your schedule. Setting boundaries, minimizing distractions, and reflecting on outcomes are essential strategies for eliminating irrelevant tasks and ensuring that your efforts drive meaningful progress toward your goals.

The importance of focus becomes more apparent, and maintaining focus on your goals is crucial for achieving success. Here is why:

Efficiency: Focusing on what matters most allows you to use your time and resources efficiently. It ensures that your efforts are directed towards tasks with the most significant impact.

Clarity: You maintain a clear vision of your objectives by ignoring the noise. This clarity helps you make better decisions and stay on track.

Progress: Consistent focus on your goals leads to steady improvement. It prevents you from getting derailed by distractions and keeps you moving forward.

What this means is you must take proactive steps to ignore the noise, and you can start by:

Set Clear Priorities: Clearly define your priorities and align your daily activities with these priorities. Use tools like to-do lists or task management apps to keep track of important tasks and deadlines.

Create a Distraction-Free Environment: Designate

a workspace that is free from distractions. This might mean setting boundaries with colleagues, turning off notifications, or using apps that block distracting websites.

Time Management Techniques: Employ time management techniques like the Pomodoro Technique, where you work in focused intervals with short breaks in between. This helps maintain concentration and productivity.

Mindfulness and Meditation: Practice mindfulness and meditation to improve focus and reduce stress. These practices help you stay present and better manage distractions.

Set Boundaries: Learn to say no to tasks and activities that do not align with your goals. Politely decline requests that divert your attention from what is essential.

Limit Information Overload: Be selective about the information you consume. Focus on sources that provide value and support your goals. Limit news and social media exposure that do not contribute to your progress.

But how does this translate to the real world, and what are some examples? Great question, and here are a few:

Workplace Focus: Imagine working on a critical project with a tight deadline. Colleagues frequently interrupt you with unrelated questions and tasks. To stay focused and let your team know you are unavailable, you can set specific times for deep work. Use noise-canceling headphones and close unnecessary tabs on your computer to minimize distractions.

Personal Goals: If you are training for a marathon, you might receive well-meaning but conflicting advice from friends and family. To stay focused, stick to a training plan from a trusted source and avoid getting sidetracked by too many opinions. Create a routine that prioritizes your training schedule and supports your goal.

Starting a Business: When launching a business, it is easy to get overwhelmed by countless opportunities and opinions. To maintain focus, create a business plan that outlines your primary objectives and strategies. Regularly review and adjust your plan, ensuring your daily activities align with your long-term goals.

You cannot ignore the role of self-discipline because ignoring the noise requires self-discipline. Here is how to cultivate it:

Develop a Routine: Establish a daily routine that supports your goals. Consistency helps build habits that keep you focused and productive.

Monitor Your Progress: Regularly review your progress toward your goals. This will help you stay accountable and make necessary adjustments to stay on track.

Reward Yourself: Recognize and reward yourself for milestones achieved. This positive reinforcement encourages continued focus and effort.

Ignoring the noise is essential for staying focused on your goals. Proactively managing distractions and maintaining a clear vision of what matters can enhance your productivity and achieve your desired outcomes. Set clear priorities, create a distraction-free environment, and practice self-discipline to stay on track.

Remember, the path to success is often cluttered with distractions and noise. Your ability to filter out these distractions and focus on your goals will determine your progress and ultimate success. Embrace the power of focus, and let it guide you towards achieving your dreams.

9

BECOME YOUR OWN CHAMPION

Today, the workforce has become highly competitive, and it is essential to recognize that you are the person who cares most about your professional accomplishments. This chapter is about taking charge of your narrative, learning to tell your story effectively, and not shying away from self-promotion. Becoming your champion means advocating for yourself, celebrating your successes, and ensuring others know your achievements.

It would be best to recognize the importance of self-promotion and why it is not bad.

Self-promotion often carries a negative connotation,

but it is vital to career success. Here's why self-promotion is essential:

Why visibility matters. In a busy work environment, individual contributions can easily be overlooked. Ensuring your hard work and achievements are visible to those who matter—such as managers, peers, and potential employers—is crucial for career advancement and personal growth. Self-promotion is not about boasting but strategically highlighting your contributions and ensuring they are recognized.

Self-promotion is necessary for several reasons. First, it helps you gain recognition for your efforts and achievements, which can lead to career advancement opportunities such as promotions, raises, and new projects. Second, it builds your brand, establishing you as a competent and reliable professional. Lastly, self-promotion increases your visibility within and outside your organization, opening doors to new opportunities and collaborations.

Just be strategic about self-promotion. Effective self-promotion requires a strategic approach. Here are some key strategies to ensure your contributions are visible and recognized.

1. Document Your Achievements - Record your accomplishments, including successful projects, milestones, and positive feedback. This documentation provides concrete evidence of your contributions and can be referenced during performance reviews, meetings, or networking opportunities. Regularly updating this record helps you stay prepared to showcase your achievements when needed.

2. Share Success Stories - Share your successes with your team and managers. Use meetings, emails, or internal communication platforms to highlight key achievements and their impact on the organization. For example, if you successfully led a project that improved efficiency or increased revenue, summarize the results and share them with relevant stakeholders. Framing your achievements in terms of their positive impact makes them more compelling and relevant.

3. Leverage Professional Networks - Use professional networking platforms like LinkedIn to share your accomplishments and insights. Regularly update your profile with new skills, certifications, and achievements. Write posts or articles about your work, industry trends, or professional experiences. Engaging with your network

enhances your visibility and positions you as a thought leader in your field.

4. Seek Out High-Visibility Projects - Actively seek opportunities to work on high-visibility projects within your organization. These projects often involve collaboration with senior leaders and can significantly boost your visibility and credibility. Volunteering for challenging assignments or cross-functional teams demonstrates your initiative and willingness to take on responsibilities.

5. Build Relationships with Influencers - Develop relationships with key influencers and decision-makers within your organization. These individuals can advocate for you and help amplify your achievements. Regularly update them on your progress and seek their feedback and support. Building a network of advocates can increase your chances of being recognized for your contributions.

6. Utilize Performance Reviews - Performance reviews are a formal opportunity to highlight your achievements and discuss your career goals. Prepare thoroughly by compiling a list of your accomplishments, the skills you have developed, and any positive feedback received. Clearly articulate how your contributions have benefited

the organization and outline your aspirations for the future.

7. Create a Personal Brand - Develop a brand that reflects your strengths, values, and professional identity. Consistently communicate this brand through your work, interactions, and online presence. A solid personal brand helps differentiate you from others and ensures your contributions are memorable and impactful.

8. Mentor and Support Others - Helping others succeed can also enhance your visibility. Offer to mentor junior colleagues, share your expertise, and contribute to team success. Your contributions are more likely to be recognized and appreciated when seen as a supportive and knowledgeable professional.

9. Present at Conferences and Events—Industry conferences, webinars, or internal company events are excellent ways to showcase your expertise and achievements. Public speaking and presentations increase your visibility and position you as a leader in your field. Seek opportunities to share your knowledge and experiences with a broader audience.

10. Solicit Testimonials and Endorsements - Ask colleagues, managers, and clients for testimonials

highlighting your strengths and accomplishments. Display these endorsements on your LinkedIn profile, personal website, or in performance reviews. Third-party validation can be robust in reinforcing your contributions and enhancing your credibility.

So, how do you overcome self-promotion challenges? Many people feel uncomfortable with self-promotion, fearing it may come across as bragging. However, self-promotion can be done professionally and respectfully. Focus on presenting facts and results rather than boasting. Emphasize the value and impact of your contributions rather than just listing accomplishments.

Visibility in a busy work environment is essential for career advancement. Self-promotion ensures that your hard work and achievements are recognized by those who matter. By documenting your achievements, sharing success stories, leveraging professional networks, seeking high-visibility projects, building relationships with influencers, utilizing performance reviews, creating a personal brand, mentoring others, presenting at events, and soliciting testimonials, you can strategically enhance your visibility and ensure that your contributions are acknowledged and valued.

A key to this is getting recognition for the work you do. Recognition is a powerful motivator and a critical factor in career advancement. Highlighting your accomplishments increases your chances of being recognized and rewarded for your hard work. Recognition can lead to promotions, raises, and new opportunities, further fueling your professional growth and success. Here is how to effectively ensure that your achievements are noticed and appreciated.

What is the importance of recognition? Recognition serves multiple purposes. It validates your efforts, boosts morale, and reinforces a sense of accomplishment. When your contributions are acknowledged, it not only enhances your confidence but also motivates you to maintain or exceed your performance levels. Recognition from peers and superiors can significantly influence your career trajectory by opening doors to advanced roles, increased responsibilities, and higher compensation.

You need to improve your ability to highlight your accomplishments. Documenting your achievements and maintaining a detailed record of them is essential. Keep track of projects you have led, targets you have achieved, and any accolades or positive feedback received. This documentation serves as tangible evidence of your contributions and can be used to support your case during performance reviews, promotion discussions, or job interviews.

Next, you need not to be shy about sharing your successes. Regularly share your achievements with your team and management. This can be done through team meetings, email updates, or internal communication platforms. When sharing, focus on the impact of your work—how it has benefited the team or the organization. For example, if you completed a project ahead of schedule or under budget, highlight how this saved resources or improved efficiency.

Take advantage of your performance reviews. No one likes year-end performance reviews, but performance reviews are formal opportunities to showcase your achievements. Prepare thoroughly by compiling a list of your key accomplishments and the skills you have developed. Use specific examples and metrics to illustrate your contributions. Articulate how your work aligns with the company's goals and has added value. This structured approach can help you make a compelling case for recognition and rewards.

Seek feedback and testimonials; they will bolster your credibility. Ask colleagues, supervisors, and clients for feedback and testimonials about your work. Positive endorsements from others can add credibility to your achievements and highlight your strengths. Display these testimonials in your performance reviews, LinkedIn profile, or personal portfolio to reinforce your contributions.

You cannot underestimate the power of networking and building relationships. Building strong relationships within your organization can increase your visibility and the likelihood of recognition. Engage with colleagues, mentors, and leaders regularly. Participate in cross-functional projects or committees to broaden your network. When people across different departments know your capabilities and contributions, it increases your chances of being recognized for new opportunities.

Remember to look outside of your company and leverage professional networks. Use professional networking platforms like LinkedIn to share your accomplishments and career milestones. Regularly update your profile with new skills, certifications, and achievements. Publishing articles or posts about your work and industry trends can further establish you as a thought leader and enhance your professional reputation.

Get uncomfortable and volunteer for high-impact or high-viability projects. Take on high-impact projects that align with your career goals and provide opportunities to showcase your skills. Volunteering for challenging assignments demonstrates your initiative and willingness to take on responsibilities. Success in these projects can lead to greater visibility and recognition from senior management.

I have done much of this and am present at conferences and events. Presenting your work at industry conferences, webinars, or internal company events effectively highlights your achievements. Public speaking and presentations increase your visibility and position you as an expert. Seek opportunities to share your knowledge and successes with a broader audience, enhancing your professional profile.

Do not just focus on yourself; celebrate team achievements. Be a team player. Recognition is not just about individual accomplishments. Celebrate team successes and acknowledge the contributions of your colleagues. By fostering a culture of mutual recognition, you create a supportive environment where everyone's efforts are valued. This strengthens team dynamics and positively reflects on your leadership and collaborative skills.

It is essential to advocate for yourself because otherwise, it will be. Do not be afraid to advocate for yourself when appropriate. If you feel your contributions are being overlooked, schedule a meeting with your supervisor to discuss your achievements and career aspirations. Communicate your desire for recognition and explain how your work aligns with the organization's goals. Self-advocacy shows that you are proactive and committed to your professional development.

What are the benefits of recognition? Recognition can lead to tangible rewards such as promotions, raises, and bonuses. It can also result in intangible benefits like increased job satisfaction, enhanced reputation, and more significant opportunities for professional growth. Recognizing your efforts reinforces your value to the organization and positions you for continued success.

Actively highlighting your accomplishments increases your chances of being recognized and rewarded. You can ensure that your hard work is noticed by documenting your achievements, sharing successes, utilizing performance reviews, seeking feedback, networking, leveraging professional platforms, volunteering for high-impact projects, presenting at events, celebrating team achievements, and advocating for yourself. Recognition validates your efforts and opens doors to promotions, raises, and new opportunities, driving your career forward.

Controlling your narrative is a powerful tool for personal and professional growth. When you tell your story, you can shape how others perceive you, highlighting your strengths, achievements, and aspirations. This self-directed narrative helps build a positive image, fosters credibility, and aligns your professional identity with your career goals.

Why Controlling Your Narrative Matters. Controlling your narrative ensures that your story is told accurately and authentically. It lets you present your achievements and skills in the best possible light, avoiding misinterpretations or undervaluing your contributions. By crafting and sharing your narrative, you can influence how colleagues, managers, potential employers, and industry peers view you, enhancing your professional reputation and opening doors to new opportunities.

Start by crafting your narrative and identifying your core strengths and achievements. Reflect on your career journey and pinpoint the skills and accomplishments that define your professional identity. Consider the projects you have successfully led, the challenges you have overcome, and the value you have added to your teams and organizations. These elements form the foundation of your narrative.

Then, define your aspirations and clearly articulate your career aspirations and long-term goals. Understanding where you want to go helps you shape your narrative to align with these objectives. For instance, if you aspire to a leadership role, emphasize your leadership experiences, strategic thinking, and ability to drive team success. Aligning your narrative with your aspirations creates a cohesive story that supports your career progression.

Remember to be authentic because authenticity is crucial in controlling your narrative. Ensure your story reflects your true self, including your values, beliefs, and personality. Authenticity builds trust and credibility, making your narrative more compelling and relatable. Share your successes and the lessons learned from challenges, as these experiences contribute to a well-rounded and genuine portrayal of your professional journey.

Use clear and compelling language and craft your narrative using clear and persuasive language. Avoid jargon and overly complex terms that might confuse your audience. Instead, focus on concise, impactful statements that effectively convey your strengths and achievements. Use specific examples and quantifiable results to illustrate your contributions and demonstrate your value.

An essential piece of this is to highlight your unique value proposition. Identify what sets you apart from others in your field. Your unique value proposition is the combination of skills, experiences, and qualities that make you an asset. Highlight this in your narrative to differentiate yourself and showcase why you are the best fit for specific roles or opportunities. For example, if you have a unique combination of technical expertise and practical communication skills, emphasize how this blend has driven your success in collaborative projects.

Then, you must be able to communicate your narrative effectively. Start with updating your professional profiles. Ensure that your professional profiles, such as LinkedIn, accurately reflect your narrative. Regularly update your profiles with new achievements, skills, and experiences. Craft a compelling headline and summary that encapsulates your strengths and aspirations. A well-maintained profile reinforces your narrative and enhances your online presence.

Creating a personal website or portfolio is also helpful. Consider creating a personal website or portfolio to showcase your work, achievements, and professional journey. This platform allows you to view your capabilities and aspirations comprehensively. Include case studies, testimonials, and detailed descriptions of your projects to provide depth to your narrative. A personal website offers a centralized location for others to learn about you and your work.

Make sure you share your story in interviews, networking events, and even online. Be prepared to share your narrative confidently when participating in interviews or networking events. Practice articulating your story to highlight your key achievements and align with the opportunities you seek. Tailor your narrative to the audience, focusing on relevant aspects of their interests and needs. Compelling storytelling in these settings can leave an impression and strengthen your professional relationships.

It is easy for anyone to publish or write a post online and to self-publish a book. Start with writing articles and speaking at events. Establish yourself as a thought leader by writing articles, blog posts, or speaking at industry events. Sharing your insights and experiences through these platforms reinforces your narrative and positions you as an expert. These activities enhance your visibility and allow you to control the narrative by presenting your ideas and achievements to a broader audience.

A common theme in this book is to seek feedback and continuously improve – you cannot stay still or static.

To refine your narrative, regularly seek feedback from trusted colleagues, mentors, and industry peers. Constructive feedback can help you identify areas for improvement and ensure that your story remains relevant and compelling. Continuously updating and improving your narrative keeps it aligned with your evolving career goals and achievements.

So, how do you overcome the challenges in controlling your narrative? How do you prevent others from creating their narrative of you?

Controlling your narrative can be challenging, especially when dealing with differing perceptions or unexpected setbacks. Stay resilient and adaptable, using challenges as opportunities to strengthen your story. Embrace a growth mindset, viewing feedback and experiences as tools for improvement. By maintaining control over your narrative, you can navigate these challenges and continue to build a positive and impactful professional image.

Controlling your narrative is essential for shaping how others perceive you and advancing your career. By crafting an authentic and compelling story highlighting your strengths, achievements, and aspirations, you can enhance your professional reputation and align your identity with your career goals. Communicate your narrative effectively through professional profiles, personal websites, interviews, networking, writing, and speaking engagements. Seek feedback and continuously improve to ensure your narrative remains relevant and robust. You can become your champion through strategic self-promotion and storytelling and achieve tremendous professional success.

This helps tell the "Story of You," learning to tell your

story effectively is crucial. Here are some steps to help you craft and communicate your narrative:

Identify Key Achievements: Reflect on your career and identify critical achievements and milestones. These could include successful projects, awards, promotions, and positive feedback from clients or colleagues.

Create a Compelling Narrative: Weave your achievements into a compelling story highlighting your journey, the challenges you overcome, and the value you bring to your role. Make sure your narrative is concise, clear, and engaging.

Use Multiple Platforms: Share your story across multiple platforms, such as your resume, LinkedIn profile, personal website, and during networking events. Tailor your message to fit the medium and audience.

Be Authentic: Authenticity is critical to effective self-promotion. Be honest about your accomplishments and the effort it took to achieve them. Authenticity builds trust and credibility.

It would be best if you overcome the fear of self-promotion. Many people hesitate to promote themselves because they fear appearing boastful or arrogant. Here is how to overcome that fear:

Reframe Self-Promotion: View self-promotion as sharing rather than bragging. You share your achievements to inspire others, highlight your contributions, and seek new opportunities.

Practice Humility: Balance your self-promotion with humility. Acknowledge the support and contributions of your team and mentors in your successes.

Prepare and Practice: Prepare how you will talk about your achievements and practice it until you are comfortable. Confidence comes with preparation and practice.

Here are some practical steps to help you promote yourself.

Update Your LinkedIn Profile: Regularly update your LinkedIn profile with new achievements, skills, and endorsements. Share articles, posts, and updates that reflect your expertise and accomplishments.

Engage in Networking: Actively participate in networking events, both online and offline. Share your story and achievements confidently and seek opportunities to connect with influencers and decision-makers in your industry.

Seek Out Speaking Opportunities: Volunteer for

speaking engagements, webinars, and panel discussions. These platforms provide excellent opportunities to showcase your expertise and share your story with a broader audience.

Request Testimonials: Ask for testimonials from colleagues, clients, and supervisors. Positive testimonials add credibility to your self-promotion efforts and provide third-party validation of your skills and accomplishments.

I'm connecting it back to real-world examples because I always find it helpful when a concept can be made clear through context.

Career Advancement: Imagine you are aiming for a promotion. Regularly update your manager on your progress and achievements. Share detailed reports on successful projects and highlight how your contributions have positively impacted the team and organization.

Entrepreneurship: If you are an entrepreneur, use your website, social media, and networking events to tell your story. Highlight your journey, the challenges you have overcome, and the successes you have achieved. This builds your brand and attracts potential clients and partners.

Job Hunting: When searching for a new job, tailor

your resume and cover letter to highlight your key achievements and strengths. During interviews, confidently discuss your past successes and how they make you an excellent fit for the role.

It would be best if you celebrated your successes – every time. Do not forget to celebrate your accomplishments, no matter how small they may seem. Here's why celebration is essential:

Boosts Confidence: Celebrating achievements, even minor ones, boosts your confidence and reinforces your self-worth.

Motivates Continued Success: Recognition and celebrating accomplishments motivate you to strive for success.

Builds a Positive Mindset: Regularly celebrating your successes helps create a positive mindset, making it easier to face challenges and setbacks.

Becoming your champion means taking charge of your career narrative and promoting your achievements. You ensure that your hard work is recognized and rewarded by effectively telling your story, overcoming the fear of self-promotion, and celebrating your successes. Remember, the person who cares most about your career is you.

Embrace the power of self-promotion, and let your story be heard.

10

BE INTENTIONAL

As we conclude this journey, it is time to reflect on the key themes we have explored and underscore the importance of intentionality. Throughout this book, we have discussed various strategies and mindsets that contribute to success, but the thread that weaves them all together is the concept of being intentional. Intentionality and determination are the cornerstone of achieving your goals and manifesting your outcomes. Let us recap some of the key themes in this book.

In most situations, you should always ask yourself why you care and to what end. We explored the importance of focusing on what truly matters to you and avoiding distractions. Understanding why you care about specific issues helps prioritize your efforts and direct your energy towards meaningful pursuits.

Remember: There is no such thing as control. We discussed the illusion of control and emphasized focusing on what you can influence. By concentrating on your actions and responsibilities, you empower yourself to make impactful changes.

Do you know what "the story of you" is? Can you tell it convincingly? Do you believe it?

Crafting and telling your narrative is crucial. Your story shapes how others perceive you and influences your professional journey. Being transparent and consistent in your story helps you navigate career transitions and reinvent yourself when necessary.

A question then is, what are you doing differently? Change requires different actions. We discussed the necessity of stepping out of your comfort zone, learning new skills, and adapting to achieve different results. Innovation and growth come from doing things differently.

The first thing you need to do is just take a step forward—it does not matter what direction. You can always change direction, but you need to start moving. It is the only way things will ever change.

Taking the first step, even without a clear direction, is essential. Action propels you forward, and each step provides valuable lessons and builds momentum towards your goals.

You need to will things into existence and manifest your outcomes.

Focus, desire, and determination are vital to achieving your dreams. Prioritizing actions that contribute to your desired outcomes while eliminating distractions ensures steady progress.

While it is hard, you must ignore the noise. Staying focused amidst distractions is vital. By proactively managing your environment and setting clear boundaries, you can maintain concentration on what truly matters.

It would be best if you became your champion. Self-promotion is essential for career success. Effectively telling your story and celebrating your achievements ensures that your hard work is recognized and opens doors to new opportunities.

But what is the essence of intentionality? Intentionality means making deliberate choices and taking purposeful actions towards your goals. It involves clarity about what you want to achieve and aligning your efforts to make it happen. Here is why being intentional is crucial:

Clarity of purpose is a cornerstone of intentional living and working. When you have a clear sense of purpose, you know exactly what you want to achieve and why it matters. This understanding directs every decision and action toward your goals, helping to eliminate distractions and maintain focus. Here is how to cultivate clarity of purpose and leverage it to drive success.

Defining Your Purpose - To achieve clarity, start by defining your purpose. Reflect on your values, passions, and long-term goals. Ask yourself what truly matters to you and what you want to accomplish personally and professionally. Your purpose should be meaningful and inspiring, providing a solid foundation for your actions and decisions.

Set Clear Goals - Once you have a clear purpose, set specific, measurable, achievable, relevant, and time-bound (SMART) goals that align with them. Clear goals break down your overarching purpose into manageable steps, providing a roadmap. For example, if your purpose is to advance in your career, set goals such as earning a relevant certification, completing a high-impact project, or achieving a promotion within a specific timeframe.

Align Actions with Purpose - Intentionality requires that your actions align with your purpose and goals. Regularly evaluate your activities to ensure they contribute to your objectives. This alignment helps prioritize tasks and focus efforts on what truly matters. For instance, if your goal is to improve your health, intentional actions might include regular exercise, a balanced diet, and sufficient sleep. Avoid activities that do not support your purpose or distract you from your goals.

Eliminate Distractions - Clarity of purpose helps identify and eliminate distractions. Knowing what you want to achieve makes it easier to recognize which activities, habits, or people are diverting you from your path. Create a focused environment by minimizing these distractions. Set boundaries, establish a dedicated workspace, and use productivity tools to stay on track. For example, limit social media use during work hours or delegate tasks not aligned with your primary goals.

Make Informed Decisions - A clear purpose guides your decision-making process. When faced with choices, consider how each option aligns with your goals. Choose paths that move you closer to your purpose and avoid those that lead you astray. This intentional decision-making ensures that your efforts are consistently directed toward achieving your objectives. For instance, if you are offered a new job opportunity, evaluate how it fits with your long-term career aspirations before deciding.

Maintain Focus and Motivation - Clarity of purpose keeps you focused and motivated. When you are clear about what you want to achieve, staying committed and resisting temptations that could derail your progress becomes more accessible. Regularly remind yourself of your purpose and the reasons behind your goals. Visualize your success and celebrate small victories along the way to maintain motivation. For example, if you want to write a book, visualize holding the finished product in your hands and celebrating each completed chapter.

Adapt to Change - While having a clear purpose is essential, it is also important to remain adaptable. Life is dynamic, and your goals may evolve. Review and reassess your purpose and objectives to ensure they remain relevant and aligned with your values. Be open to adjusting your path as needed while staying true to your core purpose. This flexibility allows you to navigate changes effectively without losing sight of your overall direction.

Seek Support and Accountability - Surround yourself with supportive individuals who understand and respect your purpose. Share your goals with trusted friends, mentors, or colleagues who can provide encouragement, advice, and accountability. Regular check-ins with these supporters can help you stay focused and motivated. For example, join a professional group or find a mentor who shares your career aspirations and can offer guidance.

Practice Self-Reflection - Regular self-reflection is crucial for maintaining clarity of purpose. Take time to reflect on your progress, challenges, and achievements. Assess whether your actions align with your goals and adjust your strategies if necessary. Self-reflection helps you stay connected to your purpose and make informed decisions about your next steps. For instance, journal about your daily accomplishments and setbacks to gain insights into your progress and areas for improvement.

Embrace a Growth Mindset - Adopting a growth mindset supports clarity of purpose by encouraging continuous learning and improvement. Embrace challenges as opportunities to grow and view setbacks as valuable learning experiences. A growth mindset helps you stay resilient and focused on your goals, even when faced with obstacles. For example, if you encounter a setback in your career, use it to develop new skills and strategies that align with your purpose.

Clarity of purpose is essential for intentional living and working. By defining your purpose, setting clear goals, aligning actions with your purpose, eliminating distractions, making informed decisions, maintaining focus and motivation, adapting to change, seeking support and accountability, practicing self-reflection, and embracing a growth mindset, you can ensure that every decision and action is geared toward achieving your goals. This clarity helps you stay focused, motivated, and resilient, leading to more tremendous success and fulfillment.

Being intentional about how you use your resources—time, energy, and money—ensures that you maximize their value and achieve your goals more effectively. Intentionality helps you focus on activities that yield the highest returns and avoid wasting effort on irrelevant tasks. Strategically managing your resources can enhance productivity, reduce stress, and drive meaningful progress.

Start with prioritizing high-impact activities. The key to efficient resource use is prioritizing activities that impact your goals most. Start by identifying which tasks and projects align most closely with your objectives. Use tools like the Eisenhower Matrix to categorize tasks by urgency and importance. Focus on activities in the "important" quadrants and delegate or eliminate those that fall into the "unimportant" categories. For example, if your goal is to advance in your career, prioritize tasks like completing a relevant certification or leading a significant project over a less impactful activity.

Ensure you optimize your time management because effective time management is essential for efficient resource use. Implement strategies such as time blocking and allocating specific time slots for focused work on high-priority tasks. Avoid multitasking, as it can dilute your focus and reduce productivity. Instead, concentrate on one task at a time to ensure high-quality outcomes. Use productivity tools like calendars, task management apps, and reminders to stay organized and on track.

Learn to delegate and outsource effectively. Recognize that you do not have to do everything yourself. Delegating tasks to others can save time and energy for more critical activities. Identify tasks that can be handled by team members, assistants, or freelancers, especially those that are time-consuming but not directly aligned with your primary goals. For instance, if you are an entrepreneur, delegating administrative tasks can allow you to focus on strategic planning and business development.

In addition to time management, one overlooked area is energy management. Managing your energy levels is just as important as managing your time. Pay attention to when you are most alert and productive, and schedule high-impact tasks during these peak periods. Take regular breaks to recharge and avoid burnout. Incorporate activities that boost your energy, such as exercise, healthy eating, and sufficient sleep, into your daily routine. You can maintain high performance and efficiency by aligning your tasks with your energy levels.

Paying attention to your monetary resources is important, whether at work or in your personal life. Being intentional with your financial resources involves investing in activities and tools that support your goals and provide a good return on investment. Avoid unnecessary expenses that do not contribute to your objectives. For example, investing in a professional course that enhances your skills and career prospects is more valuable than spending on non-essential luxuries. Regularly review your expenses to ensure they align with your priorities and adjust as needed.

Game-changing behavior is to eliminate irrelevant tasks. Eliminating irrelevant tasks is crucial for efficient resource use. These activities do not contribute to your progress and consume valuable time and energy. Conduct a regular audit of your tasks and responsibilities to identify and remove any unaligned with your goals. This process helps streamline your efforts and ensures that your resources are directed toward meaningful activities.

I am a fan of technology and utilizing technology to automate repetitive and low-value tasks. Automation tools can handle a variety of functions, from email management and social media scheduling to financial tracking and project management. By automating routine tasks, you can save time and focus on more strategic activities. For instance, using software to automate invoicing and payments can reduce administrative workload and improve efficiency.

Again, this applies to both your personal and professional life: Set clear boundaries. Setting boundaries is essential to protecting your time and energy. Learn to say no to requests and commitments that do not align with your priorities. Communicate your availability and limits to colleagues, friends, and family to avoid overextending yourself. Clear boundaries help you maintain focus and prevent distractions that can derail your progress.

I have said that you never stop learning and focus on continuous improvement. Regularly review and refine your approach to resource management. Assess what is working well and where improvements can be made. Seek feedback from mentors, peers, and team members to gain insights into how you can optimize your resource use. Embrace a continuous improvement mindset, continually seeking ways to enhance efficiency and effectiveness.

If you do not track and measure progress, are you doing anything? Monitoring and measuring your progress is vital for ensuring your resources are used efficiently. Set specific, measurable goals and monitor your achievements against these benchmarks. Use metrics and key performance indicators (KPIs) to evaluate the effectiveness of your efforts. Regular progress reviews help you identify areas where resources may be better allocated and make informed adjustments to your strategy.

Being intentional about resource use ensures that your time, energy, and financial resources are deployed efficiently to achieve your goals. Prioritize high-impact activities, optimize time and energy management, delegate and outsource tasks, eliminate irrelevant activities, leverage technology, set clear boundaries, and continuously seek improvements. Strategically managing your resources can enhance productivity, reduce stress, and drive meaningful progress, leading to tremendous success and fulfillment.

When your actions are intentional, your motivation naturally increases. This intentionality means you understand the significance of each step, fueling your drive and determination. Knowing that every action is aligned with your goals gives you a sense of purpose and keeps you focused on your desired outcomes.

Understanding the significance of each step is essential. Intentional actions are rooted in clearly understanding their importance and how they contribute to your larger goals. Knowing that every task you undertake moves you closer to your aspirations makes it easier to stay motivated. This understanding transforms routine activities into meaningful steps on your journey to success.

It would be best to start by setting meaningful goals because it is a crucial aspect of intentional action. These goals should be specific, measurable, achievable, relevant, and time-bound (SMART). When your goals are well-defined, you can see the direct connection between your daily actions and long-term objectives. This clarity provides a continuous source of motivation, as each completed task brings you one step closer to achieving your goals.

Then, you must align your actions with values. Aligning your actions with your core values enhances motivation by ensuring that your actions resonate with what you believe in. When your work reflects your values, it feels more significant and fulfilling. For example, if you value helping others, knowing that your efforts contribute to making a positive impact can drive you to work harder and stay committed.

I am a visual person, and it might be helpful if you created a visual roadmap. A visual roadmap of your goals and milestones can be a powerful motivator. This roadmap can be a vision board, a detailed project plan, or a simple checklist of tasks. Seeing your progress visually can boost your motivation by providing tangible evidence of your advancement. Each time you check off a task or reach a milestone, you receive a slight boost of accomplishment, reinforcing your determination to keep going.

I like the concept of micro goals and tend to break down goals into manageable steps. Breaking down larger goals into smaller, manageable steps makes the journey less daunting and more achievable. This approach allows you to focus on immediate tasks, reducing feeling overwhelmed. As you complete these smaller tasks, your sense of progress and achievement grows, fueling your motivation to tackle the next steps.

Do not forget to review your progress regularly. Regularly reviewing your progress helps maintain motivation by reminding you how far you have come. Schedule periodic check-ins to assess your achievements, celebrate successes, and reflect on challenges. This practice keeps you connected to your goals and allows you to adjust your strategies if needed, ensuring you remain on the right path.

It is all in your head, and cultivating a positive mindset will benefit you. A positive attitude is essential for sustaining motivation. Focus on your strengths and past successes, and view challenges as opportunities for growth. Positive self-talk and affirmations can reinforce your belief in your abilities and keep your spirits high. Surround yourself with supportive and encouraging people who uplift and motivate you.

Continuous learning and seeking inspiration can significantly enhance your motivation. Engage with resources such as books, podcasts, or workshops that inspire and educate you. Learning new skills or gaining new perspectives can reignite your passion and provide fresh motivation to pursue your goals. You are additionally seeking role models and mentors who have achieved what you aspire to and can provide valuable insights and encouragement.

Do not forget to reward yourself because incorporating rewards into your journey can boost motivation. Set up a reward system for yourself, where you treat yourself after achieving specific milestones. These rewards can be simple pleasures, such as taking a break, enjoying a favorite activity, or celebrating with friends. Rewards provide positive reinforcement and give you something to look forward to as you work towards your goals.

I believe Bruce Lee once said, be like water, and his point was you need to be flexible and adapt to win. Maintaining flexibility is critical to staying motivated in facing challenges and setbacks. Understand that the path to success is rarely linear and that adaptability is essential. When obstacles arise, view them as opportunities to learn and grow rather than insurmountable barriers. A flexible approach keeps you motivated even when plans change, or unexpected difficulties occur.

Connecting with Your "Why." Regularly reconnecting with the underlying reasons for your goals can reignite your motivation. Reflect on why you started and what you hope to achieve. Understanding your "why" provides a deep sense of purpose that can sustain you through challenging times and keep you focused on your long-term vision.

Intentional actions significantly enhance motivation by providing a clear sense of purpose and significance to each step you take. By setting meaningful goals, aligning actions with values, creating visual roadmaps, breaking down goals, regularly reviewing progress, cultivating a positive mindset, seeking inspiration, rewarding yourself, maintaining flexibility, and connecting with your "why," you can fuel your drive and determination. This intentional approach ensures that your efforts are consistently directed toward achieving your desired outcomes, leading to tremendous success and fulfillment.

Intentionality builds resilience. When setbacks occur, you are better equipped to stay on course because you have a clear vision of where you are headed and why it matters.

Intentionality is a powerful force that builds resilience, helping you stay focused and persistent even when setbacks occur. You are better equipped to navigate challenges and maintain your course when you have a clear vision of where you are headed and why it matters. Here's how intentionality fosters resilience and enables you to overcome obstacles.

A clear vision and purpose provide a solid foundation for resilience. Knowing your ultimate goals and understanding their significance gives you a sense of direction and motivation. This clarity helps you focus on the bigger picture, even when faced with difficulties. When challenges arise, your vision acts as a guiding star, reminding you what you are working towards and why it is worth the effort.

Intentionality ensures that your efforts are aligned with your goals. Concentrating on high-impact activities that contribute to your objectives maximizes your productivity and progress. This focused effort means that when setbacks happen, you have already made significant strides toward your goals, making it easier to recover and continue moving forward. Knowing your purposeful and meaningful actions strengthens your determination to overcome obstacles.

Being intentional involves planning and anticipating potential challenges. This proactive approach allows you to develop adaptive strategies to address setbacks effectively. When you encounter a problem, you can quickly pivot and implement alternative solutions without losing sight of your goals. This flexibility and preparedness enhance your ability to handle disruptions and maintain progress.

Intentionality fosters a positive mindset, which is crucial for resilience. When intentional about your actions, you focus on solutions rather than dwelling on problems. This positive outlook helps you see setbacks as temporary, surmountable, rather than insurmountable barriers. A positive mindset encourages you to learn from challenges and view them as opportunities for growth and improvement.

Intentionality builds self-confidence by reinforcing belief in your abilities and commitment to your goals. Each intentional action and achievement boosts your confidence, making you more resilient in adversity. When setbacks occur, you can draw on this confidence to persevere, knowing you have the skills and determination to overcome obstacles.

Being intentional about your relationships and support systems also contributes to resilience. Surrounding yourself with supportive and encouraging individuals provides a network of allies who can offer guidance, motivation, and assistance during tough times. Intentionality in building these relationships ensures that you have a reliable support system to lean on when needed.

Regular reflection and adjustment are vital components of intentionality that enhance resilience. By routinely evaluating your progress and strategies, you can identify areas for improvement and make necessary adjustments. This ongoing process of reflection helps you stay agile and responsive to changes, enabling you to navigate setbacks more effectively. It also reinforces your commitment to your goals as you continually refine your approach to achieve better outcomes.

Intentionality involves efficient resource management, which is vital for resilience. By wisely allocating your time, energy, and financial resources, you ensure you can handle setbacks without being overwhelmed. Effective resource management allows you to maintain momentum and stay focused on your goals, even when unexpected challenges arise.

Intentionality encourages a growth mindset, where setbacks are viewed as valuable learning experiences. Each challenge provides insights that can inform future actions and decisions. By analyzing setbacks and extracting lessons from them, you become better equipped to handle similar situations in the future. This continuous learning process strengthens your resilience and enhances your problem-solving abilities.

Intentionality involves a solid commitment to long-term goals. This commitment provides the persistence needed to weather setbacks and stay on course. When deeply committed to your goals, you are more likely to push through difficulties and remain focused on achieving your vision. This unwavering dedication is a hallmark of resilience.

Celebrating small victories and progress reinforces your intentional efforts and builds resilience. Recognizing and appreciating your achievements, no matter how minor, boosts your morale and motivation. These celebrations remind you of your capabilities and progress, encouraging you to keep going despite setbacks.

Intentionality builds resilience by providing a clear vision and purpose, focusing efforts, developing adaptive strategies, fostering a positive mindset, building self-confidence, cultivating support systems, encouraging regular reflection and adjustment, managing resources efficiently, learning from setbacks, maintaining commitment to long-term goals, and celebrating progress. This intentional approach equips you to handle challenges effectively, stay on course, and achieve your desired outcomes, no matter your obstacles.

Practical Steps to Being More Intentional

What are the practical steps to be intentional? It is a lot easier than you think.

Set Clear Goals: Define your goals with precision. Use the SMART criteria to ensure your goals are Specific,

Measurable, Achievable, Relevant, and Time-bound. Clear goals provide a roadmap for your actions.

Develop a Plan: Create a detailed plan that outlines the steps needed to achieve your goals. This plan should include timelines, milestones, and resources required. A well-structured plan acts as a guide, keeping you on track.

Prioritize Actions: Focus on high-impact actions that move you closer to your goals. Prioritize tasks that align with your objectives and delegate or eliminate those that do not.

Regularly Review and Adjust: Review your progress and plan as needed. Stay flexible and be willing to adapt your approach based on new information and changing circumstances.

Stay Committed: Maintain your commitment to your goals. Stay disciplined and avoid getting sidetracked by short-term distractions. Remember why you started and keep your eyes on the long-term vision.

Success does not happen accidentally; it results from intentional actions and determined effort. Throughout this book, we have explored various strategies to help you navigate your career and personal growth. The common thread is the importance of being intentional in everything you do.

By being intentional, you harness your focus, align your efforts, and drive your actions toward meaningful outcomes. This deliberate approach to life and work enhances your chances of success and ensures that your journey is purposeful and fulfilling.

As you move forward, remember that intentionality and determination breed success. Embrace the power of intention, take deliberate actions, and remain steadfast in your pursuit of excellence. Your future is shaped by your choices today, so make them with intention and watch as you achieve your dreams.

ABOUT THE AUTHOR

Frank Lazaro is a seasoned executive, accomplished inventor, and technology enthusiast passionate about driving profitable growth through innovative products and services. With over 20 years of marketing, technology, and strategy experience, Frank has established himself as a purposeful global executive, distinguished by his impressive portfolio of US patents for business processes and product design.

Frank has held critical positions at world-renowned brands such as Deloitte, AT&T, and Fiserv (formerly First Data), gaining invaluable experience across multiple industries, sectors, and verticals. His natural talent for creating and marketing products that build revenue has led him to build highly effective teams and programs that have consistently delivered exceptional results. His dedication to technology and its transformative power has helped him stay ahead of the curve, continually innovating in a fast-paced, ever-changing industry.

Frank is a dynamic leader with a proven track record of delivering results through innovation, strategic planning, and effective team management. His passion for technology and creating solutions that drive growth is unmatched, making him an asset to any organization. Frank is a visionary in the AEC industry and a trailblazer in artificial intelligence within the AEC space. Drawing from his experience and unique insights, Frank has bridged the gap between traditional AEC practices and innovative AI-driven methodologies.

Frank's influence extends beyond the AEC industry into financial services, where his vision and passion have driven significant advancements. His commitment to sharing knowledge is evident in his written works. His books, such as "AEC Marketer's Guide to Artificial Intelligence" and "Let Me Be Frank with You," testify to his depth of understanding and ability to connect with readers. Through his writings and initiatives, Frank aspires to shape the future of the AEC industry by blending creativity with innovative technology.

Frank's academic foundation, fortified with an MBA, underscores his deep-rooted passion for and dedication to the evolving landscape of artificial intelligence. His journey, enriched with significant achievements in technology and strategy, showcases his profound expertise in harnessing AI's transformative power across diverse sectors.

As an accomplished inventor, Frank's portfolio of US patents highlights his creative prowess and forward-thinking approach to AI applications in business processes and product design. Beyond his technical accomplishments, Frank is an acclaimed author, having penned works that highlight his commitment to demystifying AI and sharing his extensive knowledge, aiming to empower a broader audience with the skills to navigate and excel in the AI-driven future.

Frank's unique blend of technical innovation, strategic vision, and educational outreach positions him as a leading voice in the AI community. He inspires professionals and enthusiasts alike to explore the vast potential of artificial intelligence. His enthusiasm for AI technology and learning is evident in his professional engagements and community services, where he continuously influences and inspires his environment.

Frank is a visionary leader, innovator, and author whose expertise in AI and technology has positioned him at the forefront of multiple industries. His dedication to sharing knowledge and driving growth through innovative solutions makes him an invaluable asset to any organization. Through his books, leadership, and ongoing initiatives, Frank continues to shape the future of the AEC industry and beyond, blending creativity with innovative technology to achieve exceptional results.

APPENDIX

Creating a list of references and sources for this book's content is somewhat challenging since the material consists of my opinions, general advice, and common knowledge on productivity, goal-setting, and personal development rather than specific, cited sources.

However, I can provide a list of influential books, articles, and thought leaders that align with the principles discussed in the content. These sources can serve as further reading and context for the ideas presented:

Books on Productivity and Goal-Setting:

> "The 7 Habits of Highly Effective People" by Stephen R. Covey: This book discusses principles of personal and professional effectiveness, including the importance of goal-setting and prioritization.

> "Atomic Habits" by James Clear: Focuses on building good habits, breaking bad ones, and the impact of small changes on achieving significant goals.

> "Getting Things Done: The Art of Stress-Free Productivity" by David Allen: Offers a comprehensive system for managing tasks and projects efficiently.

Books on Resilience and Growth Mindset:

"Grit: The Power of Passion and Perseverance" by Angela Duckworth: Explores the role of grit and resilience in achieving long-term goals.

"Mindset: The New Psychology of Success" by Carol S. Dweck: Introduces the concept of fixed versus growth mindsets and their impact on learning and success.

Books on Time Management:

"Deep Work: Rules for Focused Success in a Distracted World" by Cal Newport: Discusses strategies for achieving deep, focused work and minimizing distractions.

"The Pomodoro Technique" by Francesco Cirillo: Describes a time management method that uses timed intervals to boost productivity.

Books on Self-Promotion and Personal Branding:

"Me 2.0: 4 Steps to Building Your Future" by Dan Schawbel: Focuses on personal branding and how to market oneself effectively in a competitive job market.

"Brag!: The Art of Tooting Your Own Horn without Blowing It" by Peggy Klaus: Offers strategies for self-promotion without appearing boastful.

Books on Intentional Living:

"Essentialism: The Disciplined Pursuit of Less" by Greg McKeown: Advocates for focusing on what truly matters and eliminating the non-essential.

"The One Thing: The Surprisingly Simple Truth Behind Extraordinary Results" by Gary Keller and Jay Papasan: Emphasizes the importance of focusing on the single most important task to achieve success.

Articles and Thought Leaders:

Harvard Business Review: Regularly publishes articles on productivity, goal-setting, and personal development.

James Clear's Blog: Provides insights on habits, decision-making, and continuous improvement.

Cal Newport's Blog: Focuses on deep work, digital minimalism, and productivity strategies.

Tools and Techniques:

Eisenhower Matrix: A time management tool used to prioritize tasks by urgency and importance.

SMART Goals Framework: A widely used framework for setting clear and achievable goals.

FRANK LAZARO

www.ingramcontent.com/pod-product-compliance
Lightning Source LLC
Chambersburg PA
CBHW071217090426
42736CB00014B/2857